Bible Wars On the Horizon

Are Prophesied Wars Approaching?

by

Al Gist

Copyright © 2014 by Al Gist

Bible Wars On the Horizon - Are Prophesied Wars Approaching?

Printed in the U.S.A.

ISBN-13:
978-1502523488
ISBN-10:
1502523485

All rights reserved solely by the author. No part of this book may be reproduced in any form without permission of the author.

Unless otherwise indicated, Bible quotations are taken from The King James Version.

www.maranathaevangelisticministries.com
email: al_gist@hotmail.com

Table of Contents

Introduction……………………………………………… 4

Lesson 1 - The Blood Red Moons……………..………… 5
    Lesson 1 Quiz……………………….………..………… 31

Lesson 2 - ISIS, Damascus, and the Prophecy of Isaiah 17…. 33
    Lesson 2 Quiz……………………………………….…... 53

Lesson 3 - The War of Gog of Magog – Part 1……………… 55
    Lesson 3 Quiz……………………………………….…... 66

Lesson 4 - The War of Gog of Magog – Part 2……………… 68
    Lesson 4 Quiz……………………………………….…... 82

Lesson 5 - The War of Gog of Magog – Part 3……………… 84
    Lesson 5 Quiz……………………………………….…... 99

Introduction

The Middle East is in complete turmoil. Libya, Egypt, Iraq, Syria, and Lebanon are all suffering from civil strife and governmental upheaval. Iran is still exporting weapons to terrorist groups and pushing ahead with their program to build their own nuclear arsenal. ISIS (The Islamic State of Iraq and Syria) has risen from the anarchy in Syria as the world's most brutal terrorist organization and has now captured parts of Syria and Iraq in its quest to establish an Islamic Caliphate throughout the Middle East.

In the midst of all this fighting and chaos lies the tiny nation of Israel which is busy fighting Hamas in Gaza and other Palestinian terrorists in the West Bank. So the heat is rising on Israel, from within and from without (all around). Is the stage being set for another Arab-Israeli war? Do the blood red moons of this year and next point to such a war?

In this lesson series, we will begin with a study of "The Blood Red Moons", a phenomenon that some believe is pointing to an imminent major hardship upon Israel, perhaps another war. Then, we will look at some prophesied end time wars spoken of in the Bible and how the current fighting in the Middle East and in eastern Europe could possibly be leading up to those wars.

The aim of this study is to increase the student's awareness to the possible connections of these current events and what God's prophetic Word tells us about the last days of the Church Age. Being cautious to not "force fit" today's headlines into the fulfillment of Bible prophecy, we do want to encourage people to look at them through the lens of Scripture. Only God knows the future and thus, our knowledge of what lies ahead must be established on what is written in the Bible. With that approach, the wise student of God's Word will be alerted (without sensationalism) to the nearness of the Rapture of the Church and to be active in God's Kingdom work in these last days.

Lesson 1
The Blood Red Moons

In talking about the great day of our Lord's Second Coming, when He will burst upon the inhabitants of this earth riding a great, white stallion as the King of Kings, God says through the prophet Joel…

Joel 2:30 - *And I will shew wonders in the heavens and in the earth, blood, and fire, and pillars of smoke.*
31 **The sun shall be turned into darkness, and the moon into blood**, **before** *the great and the terrible day of the LORD come.*

In this lesson, we will look at some very unusual astronomical phenomenon that are upon us now known as "The Blood Red Moons" and what (if any) prophetic significance they may have. But first, in order for us to understand it, we need to make a short study of the **Seven Annual Feasts of Israel.**

In Lev. 23, God instituted seven annual feasts that the Jewish people were to observe. Each feast served to help the Israelites remember something that God had done for them.

For example, the first feast of the year is Passover. The purpose of the Passover Feast was to commemorate the day when the death angel "passed over" the houses of the Jewish people who had put the blood of the lamb on the door posts and over the top of the front door of their house. In all of the homes that did not have the blood applied, the first born child died. And it was through this plague that the Pharaoh was finally forced to allow the Israelites to leave Egypt. Likewise, each of the Seven Feasts of Israel were to commemorate something that God did for the Jews.

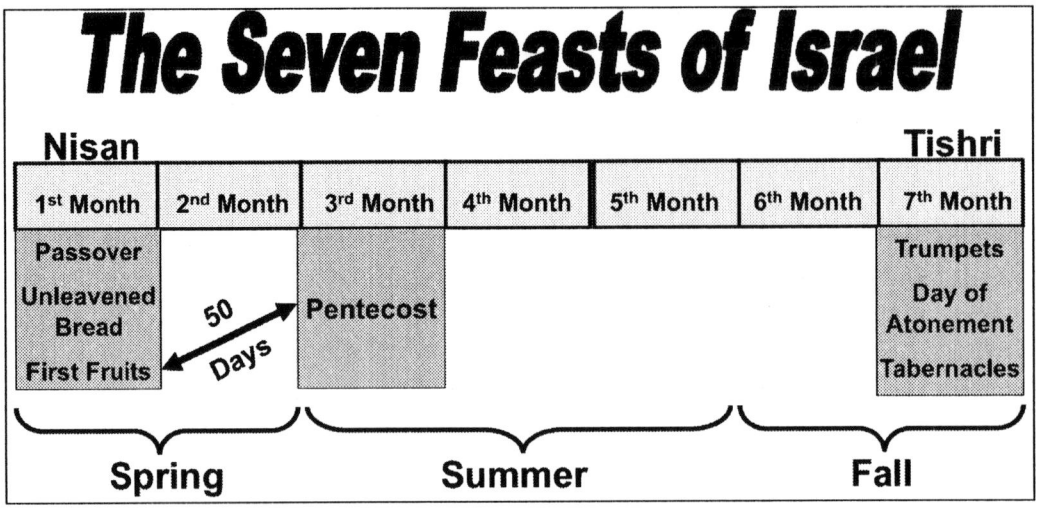

The Feasts are observed at three times of the year… three in the Spring, one in the Summer, and then three in the Fall:

- Passover, Unleavened Bread, and Firstfruits were observed in the Spring.
- Fifty days later in the early Summer was the Feast of Pentecost.
- Trumpets, Day of Atonement, and Tabernacles were observed in the Fall.

When Jesus came to this earth, He said,

Matt 5:17 - *Think not that I am come to destroy the law* [about the observance of the feasts], *or the prophets: I am not come to destroy,* **but to fulfill**.

A study of the Seven Feasts will show that Jesus has **already fulfilled** the first four of the Seven Feasts.
- He died on Passover as the Passover Lamb of God.
- He was buried on Unleavened Bread as the Bread of Life.
- He arose from the grave on the following Sunday, the day of the Feast of Firstfruits, as He became the firstfruit of many more to be resurrected unto eternal life.

- Fifty days later, on the Day of Pentecost, He sent the Holy Spirit to indwell the Church.

Just as He fulfilled the first four feasts ON THE DAY of their observance, in the order in which they were observed, it makes sense to think that He will fulfill the last three on the day of their observance and in the order of their observance. HOW He will fulfill them, only God knows…

But the next feast is the Feast of Trumpets and it is observed with the blowing of trumpets. It is POSSIBLE that He will fulfill that one by rapturing the Church… when

1 Thess 4:16 - *…the Lord himself shall descend from heaven with a shout, with the voice of the archangel, and **with the trump of God**: and the dead in Christ shall rise first:*
17 Then we which are alive and remain shall be caught up together with them in the clouds, to meet the Lord in the air: and so shall we ever be with the Lord.

We don't KNOW that that is the way the Lord is going to fulfill the Feast of Trumpets, but it's possible… and it makes sense.

Also, He MAY fulfill **the Day of Atonement** with His Second Coming when He will save the Jews from annihilation at the end of the Tribulation. As Zechariah says,

Zech 13:1 - *In that day there shall be a fountain opened to the house of David and to the inhabitants of Jerusalem for sin and for uncleanness.*

So, He will atone for His Jewish brethren as they turn to Him en masse as their true Messiah and Savior.

And, then finally, He will probably fulfill the **Feast of Tabernacles** by "tabernacling" with the Redeemed for 1000 years in His Millennial Kingdom.

So, the Lord fulfilled the three spring feasts in **His First Coming** and then He inaugurated the Church Age on Pentecost. Following that is the long time of the Church Age and then He will fulfill the last three feasts at **His Second Coming**.

I want to make it perfectly clear that I am not trying to set a date for the Rapture of the Church by suggesting that it may happen on the Feast of Trumpets! No one knows exactly WHEN the Rapture is going to occur... and, it COULD happen at any moment.

However, what I *am* giving you is "food for thought". I want you to be aware of these things. And I am NOT being dogmatic about it because the truth is that even with all of the seeming connections of the Rapture to the Feast of Trumpets with the blowing of trumpets, we can only conclude with certainty that those are just *possible* connections.

And what about the year? Even if the Rapture does occur on Trumpets... what *year* will it occur? We don't know. But, TODAY, there are many signs being fulfilled that tell us that we are living in the end of the Church Age. We are living in *the last of the Last Days*. So, even though we cannot know the actual DAY that Jesus will come for His Church, we *can* say with certainty that we are now living in the **SEASON OF HIS COMING!**

And what I am going to show you next may be another INDICATOR of that. Even the planets appear to be pointing to the nearness of His coming!

When Jesus was giving His Olivet Discourse and He was talking about the days of the Tribulation, He said in verse 29…

Matt 24:29 - *Immediately **AFTER** the tribulation of those days shall the sun be darkened, and the moon shall not give her light, and the stars shall fall from heaven, and the powers of the heavens shall be shaken:*

Now, the "stars falling from heaven" is likely a reference to an immense meteorite shower. But for years, like most Bible students, I thought that the idea of "the sun being darkened and the moon not giving her light", was some supernatural phenomenon where God miraculously causes the light of these celestial bodies to cease momentarily… just as He did from 12:00 noon to 3:00 PM on the day Jesus was crucified (Matt. 27:45).

But, maybe Jesus was not referring to some ***supernatural*** occurrence, but rather to a NATURAL occurrence. Maybe it was a reference to ***eclipses*** because a solar eclipse causes darkness to fall upon the earth as the moon passes between the earth and the sun. And the moon, instead of shining, appears as a "black ball" blocking out the light of the sun.

So, was the Lord saying that the days immediately AFTER The Tribulation, just before He returns "with power and great glory", will be marked by solar and lunar eclipses and meteorite showers? That is certainly a possibility.

Well, let's look at some other Scriptures that associate these astronomical phenomenon with the Lord's Coming. But first, let me explain the term "Day of the Lord"…

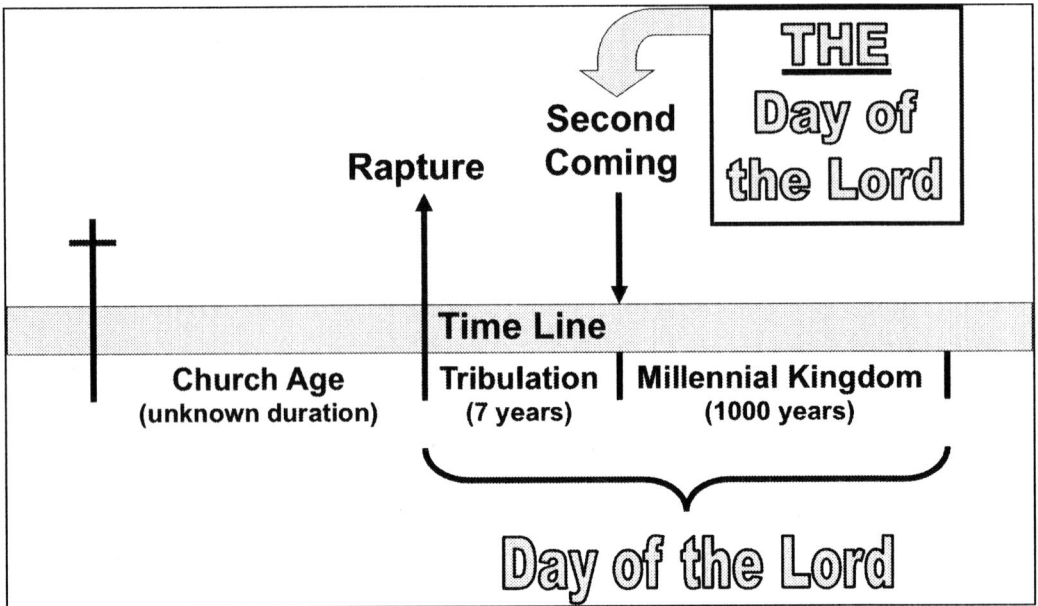

There is a time *period* that will be the "Day of the Lord" and it will begin with the Tribulation and go all the way through the time of the Millennial Kingdom. However, there is also a *specific* "Day of the Lord" (a 24-hr. day) when the Lord will come in great wrath and power at His Second Coming to destroy the enemies of God at the end of the Tribulation.

Now, let's look at three other Scriptural references to that great and terrible day of the Lord at His Second Coming, when the light of the sun and the moon will be darkened.

(1) This first one is found in Isaiah, but this one does not sound like a reference to eclipses…

Isa 13:9 - *"Behold, the day of the LORD cometh, cruel both with wrath and fierce anger, to lay the land desolate: and he shall destroy the sinners thereof out of it.*
10 For the stars of heaven and the constellations thereof shall not give their light: **the sun shall be darkened in his going forth, and the moon shall not cause her light to shine***."*

Here, Isaiah gives us a description of how the STARS will not shine, and the sun will be darkened, as well as the moon. This sounds much more like the blotting out of ***all*** the lights of the sky. And, of course, God could do that supernaturally, or He could do it through more natural means.

For instance, scientists tell us that with the explosion of an atomic bomb, thousands of tons of dust and debris are blown into the sky causing a dust cloud in the upper atmosphere. In a war with many such explosions, an eerie haze would form that could encircle the planet blocking out the light of the sun, moon, and stars. With the widespread warfare in the last half of the Tribulation, there will most likely be NUCLEAR wars that could cause this to happen.

So, with the inclusion of the darkening of the STARS (which could not be the result of an eclipse), this Isaiah passage does not appear to be a reference to eclipses and I would not include it with the idea of "blood red moons" or lunar and solar eclipses.

Isaiah does not give us a relative time reference about all of this happening, only that it's associated with "the day of the Lord." So, this "darkening of the sky" could happen during the latter days of the Tribulation leading up to the Second Coming.

But, now lets go back to Joel.

(2) Listen again to what the prophecy of Joel 2 says about it…

Joel 2:31 - " ***The sun shall be turned into darkness, and the moon into blood**, **before*** *the great and the terrible day of the LORD come."*

Joel is very specific that this darkening of the sun and moon's light will happen BEFORE the Lord's Second Coming. But again, he doesn't say HOW LONG before.

The Apostle Peter confirmed this last days phenomenon on the day of Pentecost, when he stood up to preach. He spoke of that last day when the Lord will come in power and glory quoting the passage from Joel:

Acts 2:17a - *"And it shall come to pass **in the last days**, saith God…*
19   *…I will shew wonders in heaven above, and signs in the earth beneath; blood, and fire, and vapour of smoke:*
20   ***The sun shall be turned into darkness, and the moon into blood, BEFORE that great and notable day of the Lord come****:* [or we could say… BEFORE the Second Coming happens]*"*

So although Joel prophesied mostly about the coming destruction by the Babylonians, it is obvious that his prophecies would have a dual fulfillment in the end of time. As previously mentioned, many centuries later, Peter spoke of it on Pentecost as though it would be fulfilled in those future "last days" just before the Lord's Second Coming. So, this must be what Joel meant when he said that it will happen *"**BEFORE** that great and terrible day of the Lord come"*.

Again, what he does NOT tell us is HOW FAR BEFORE the Lord's Second Coming that this will happen. But since it is associated with the Lord's Second Coming, it is obviously something that will happen in the relative proximity to it... perhaps even sometime in the last decade leading up to it. But we need not assign it to THE DAY BEFORE the Lord's coming.

(3) In the Revelation, with the opening of the sixth seal, it says this:

Rev 6:12 - *"And I beheld when he had opened the sixth seal, and, lo, there was a great earthquake; and the* **sun became black as sackcloth of hair, and the moon became as blood;***"*

Here, the Scripture talks about a great earthquake and goes on to say that the people of the earth hid themselves in caves and the rocks of the mountains... crying out for the mountains and rocks to hide them from *"the wrath of the Lamb... For the great day of His wrath is come; and who shall be able to stand?"* (Rev 6:16-17) This is one of the last "bowl judgments" of God that is poured out on earth in the last half of the Tribulation. So, these celestial phenomenon are obviously a reference to a time BEFORE the Second Coming.

So, there are a number of Scriptures that speak of the sun becoming dark and the moon becoming red at the time of... (or, just before) the Second Coming of our Lord when He will destroy the enemies of God.

Now, when we look at the Genesis account of creation, when God put the planets in their orbits, Genesis 1:14 says...

Gen 1:14 - *"And God said, Let there be lights in the firmament of the heaven to divide the day from the night* [so the revolving of our planet creates the cycle of day and night]; *and let them be for* **signs,** *and for seasons, and for days, and years:"*

We can easily understand what it means when it says that the planets in their orbits are used to determine the "days and years". Our calendar days and years are established by the spinning of the earth on its axis (one day) and by its orbit around the sun (one year). But what does it mean when it speaks of "signs and seasons"?

The Hebrew word translated here as "signs" is "owth", meaning "a signal". So, God uses the planets to "signal" us. But we must be watching for the signal or it won't mean anything!

The word translated as "seasons" here does NOT mean summer, fall, winter, and spring. In fact, it is the exact same word used for **"feasts" in Lev. 23**. When we think of feasts, we think of food, but in the Hebrew, it is the word **"mowed"**, and it has nothing at all to do with food. It actually means **"appointments"**. God set seven annual **"appointments"** with the Jewish people when they were to turn away from their daily routines and meet with Him!

So, the planets were put in their orbits to *signal* us about certain *appointed* times… just as the star over Bethlehem was used to **signal** the wise men of that special, **appointed time**, the birth of our Lord Jesus.

Luke tells us that before the Lord comes, the celestial bodies will give "signs" of the His imminent coming:

Luke 21:25 - *"And there shall be **signs in the sun, and in the moon, and in the stars**…*

27 ***And then shall they see the Son of man coming in a cloud with power and great glory.***"

Historians of the past centuries would sometimes note certain historical events by attaching them to a solar or lunar eclipse that took place at that time.
(NASA web page http://eclipse.gsfc.nasa.gov/LEhistory/LEhistory.html)

If one accepts that God has foreordained the major events of history, then it's easy to see how He could *signal* an *appointed time* for something to happen in history by the appearance of an eclipse! In fact, we might even think of the planets in our solar system as God's Great Clock. Knowing the exact time of every historical event at the time of creation, God set the planets in their precise orbits in such a way that they would designate the timing of those events.

And today, we know that if something happened on the date of a particular eclipse, we can know that exact date. The timing of eclipses in both the past and the future can be precisely calculated. In fact, you can go to the NASA web site (which I did) and it will give you the dates and times of all the solar and lunar eclipses for the last 4000 years and the next 2000 years! What a great way for God to pinpoint events on the timeline of history for us (using His Great Clock)!

So, it appears that even as historians have used eclipses to designate the date of some world events, God tells us that that is the way He intended it to be. He put the earth and the moon in their exact orbits in a way that their positions would denote special historical events that He foreordained in the timeless past. Or, another way of saying it is, He has scheduled certain events in history to happen at specific times, and those times have coincided with the eclipses!

Basically, there are two kinds of eclipses:

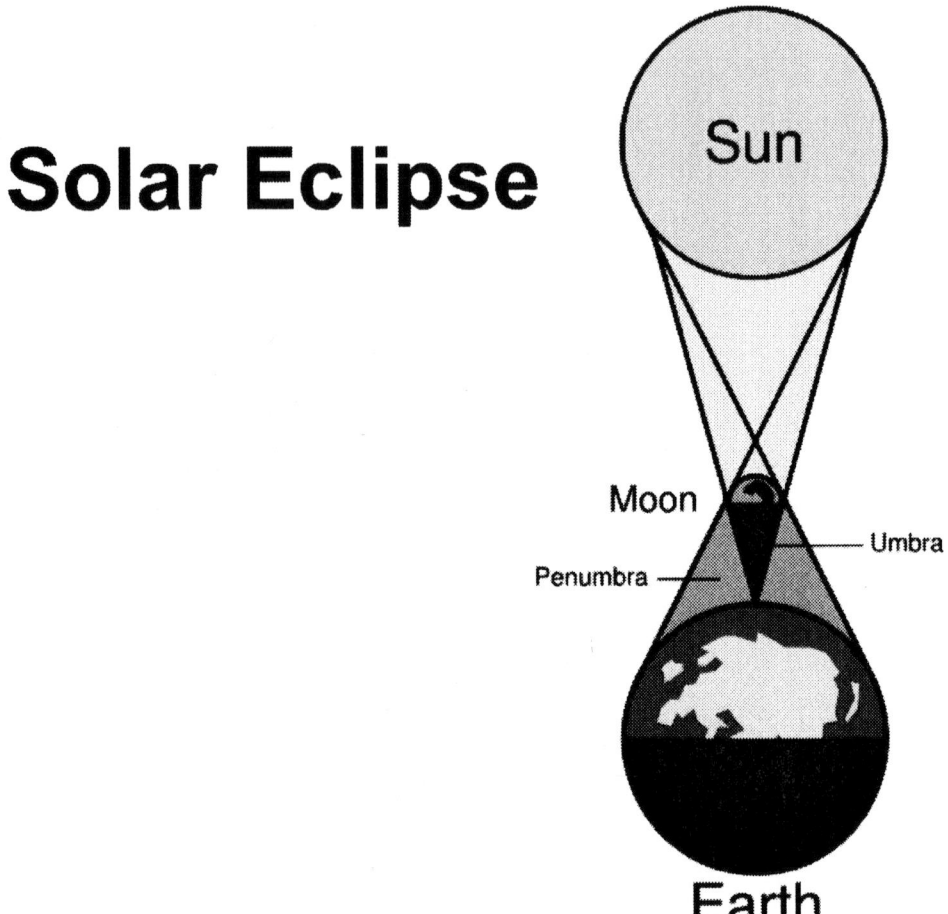

(1) There are **solar eclipses** where the moon gets between the earth and the sun and blocks the light of the sun.

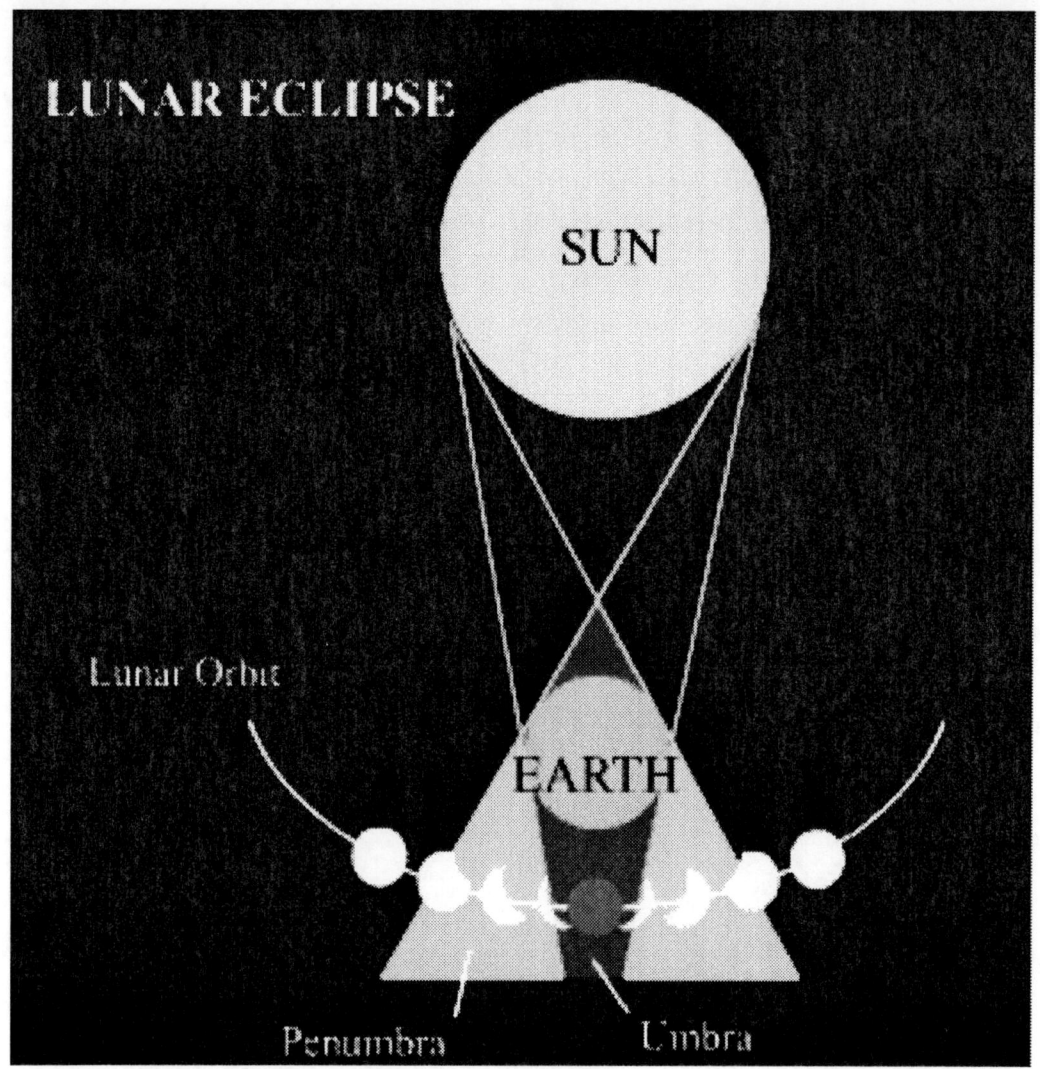

(2) And there are **lunar eclipses** where the earth gets between the sun and the moon and casts its shadow on the moon. In a ***total*** lunar eclipse, because the earth is surrounded by atmospheric gases which diffuse the sun's light, the earth's shadow on the moon is a reddish hue causing the moon to become "red as blood". So, a "blood red moon" is simply a reference to total lunar eclipse.

Now, according to Jewish tradition, *lunar* eclipses occur on some great historical event that has to do with Israel (or the Jews). (see http://thetruthwins.com/archives/the-blood-red-moons-of-2014-and-2015-an-omen-of-war-for-israel). **Solar** eclipses portend a great historical event among the Gentile nations.

Let's talk about the lunar eclipses first…

On the NASA web site, I discovered that the occurrence of a **total** lunar eclipse (blood red moon) is *not* such an unusual event. In fact, in this century, there will be a total of 228 *lunar* eclipses. Some of those will be *partial eclipses.* But out of those 228, 85 will be *total eclipses.* [3] So that's an average of just under one per year.

But when we have **two total lunar eclipses back-to-back** (without any partial eclipses in between), that's a little more unusual. There are six of those that are supposed to happen in this century.

And, of course if you have *three* total lunar eclipses back-to-back, that's even more unusual. There will be 12 of those in this century.

But when you have *four* **consecutive total lunar eclipses back-to-back**, this is pretty rare. Four total lunar eclipses in a row like that is what scientists call a **TETRAD**. And even though tetrads are pretty rare, there are 8 of them that are supposed to happen in this century.

There were:
5 Tetrads in 1901-2000
Before that, there were NONE in the 1800s…
NONE in the 1700s…
And NONE in the 1600s.

Going back in history, the next one we see is in the years 1580-1581 and it turns out that there were six of them in the 1500s..

So, TETRADS (four consecutive total lunar eclipses... or, four "blood red moons") are pretty unusual. But what do you think the chances would be for a tetrad to occur where each of the four "blood red moons" fall exactly on a Jewish feast day? Now, THAT would be an interesting phenomenon! For lack of a better name, I'm going to call that a "FEAST DAY TETRAD".

Well, it just so happens that "Feast Day Tetrads" DO occur... but not very often. In this century, there will only be ONE... (We'll talk more about that one in just a moment.) Out of the five tetrads in the last century, it was very unusual.... But ***two of them were "Feast Day Tetrads"!!!***

So, do you know when the two "Feast Day Tetrads" occurred in the last century?

- The last one was in the years 1967-1968. June, 1967 was the Six Day War when Israel captured their holy city, Jerusalem.
- The one before that was in the years 1949-1950. Israel declared her independence on May 14, 1948. She was attacked the next day (May 15, 1948) by five Arab nations. And her War of Independence was won in ***early 1949*** when the Armistice Agreements were signed. So, in 1949, she won her War of Independence and stood with secure borders as an independent nation.

So, the first Feast Day Tetrad last century fell on the year that Israel won her War of Independence. And the second Feast Day Tetrad occurred when Israel won the Six Day War and captured Jerusalem.

To see another "Feast Day Tetrad", we have to go all the way back to the year 1492. Of course, 1492 was when "Columbus sailed the ocean blue" and discovered America. But that is also the year that the Jews were expelled from Spain during the days of the horrible Spanish Inquisition. And many thousands who did not flee for their lives were executed. To this day, the horrors suffered by the Jews in Spain in 1492 are remembered.

So, off-hand, I would say that the "Feast Day Tetrads"(at least the last three… the ones that have occurred in the last 600 years) seem to **roughly** coincide with some cataclysmic historical event related to the Jews.

Now, I said earlier that there is going to be ONLY ONE "Feast Day Tetrad" in this century. Well, it's going to happen in the years 2014-2015!

As I showed you earlier, the first feast of the Jewish year is **Passover**… And the last feast of the year is **Tabernacles**. What's really interesting is that on the *exact* dates of Passover and Tabernacles in 2014… AND on the *exact* dates of Passover and Tabernacles in 2015, there will be four consecutive, total lunar eclipses… four "blood red moons". In other words, this year and next, **four consecutive "blood red moon" total lunar eclipses will fall exactly on the dates of Passover and Tabernacles.**

The dates for these four lunar eclipses are:
Passover – April 15, 2014
Tabernacles – Oct. 8, 2014

Passover – April 4, 2015
Tabernacles – Sept. 28, 2015

Now, what is the significance of *this* Feast Day Tetrad? If it is going to happen at a time of special prophetic significance, exactly WHAT HISTORICAL EVENT is it pointing to? The answer to that is, "I DON'T KNOW." Nor, does anyone else know! Remember, only God knows the future.

Some are trying to say that the Rapture will happen in the time frame of this Feast Day Tetrad. But there is no way that they can know that! It certainly COULD happen during that time, but the truth is that it could happen at *any* time… even five minutes from now, or five years from now.

But, there are **two points** that I want to make about the significance of *this* Feast Day Tetrad:

1. It probably is NOT *directly* related to the Rapture of the Church. Why? Because the Feast Days are **Jewish** holy days. They don't have anything to do with the Church. And the Rapture is a "Church Event", NOT a Jewish event.

And, if we look at the historical record, it appears that (at least) the last three Feast Day Tetrads coincided with major hardships on the Jewish people followed by a blessing:

- Their expulsion from Spain in 1492 was a terrible hardship. Thousands of them were executed with horrible means of torture. BUT, it was that same year that Columbus sailed for America, which eventually led to a nation that would become a great safe haven for Jews and the greatest supporter of their eventual re-establishment as a nation.

- Their war of Independence in 1948-49 was another terrible hardship. Tens of thousands of them died in battle against the Arabs, but it resulted in the great blessing that they were established as an independent and sovereign nation.

- Their Six Day War in 1967 was a terrible hardship. But it led to their taking the entire city of Jerusalem, their eternal capital city, which they hold to this day… another hardship followed by a blessing.

So, I totally disagree with those who may be trying to pinpoint the Rapture of the Church by saying that it is going to happen on one of the feast days in this Feast Day Tetrad. Or, even that it will definitely happen sometime during this Feast Day Tetrad. There is no way that we can know WHEN the Rapture is going to happen. And the Feast Day Tetrads seem to have **_more to do_** with the Jews than with the Church.

But if the trend of the last three Feast Day Tetrads continues, then this Feast Day Tetrad is pointing to some major hardship on Israel (like another war), but it will undoubtedly result in some major blessing (victory in that war).

Now, there are Bible prophecies of at least a couple of **last days wars** against Israel (depending on your interpretation of these things) that will happen either just before, or in the first half of the Tribulation.

   a. One is the Psalm 83 War that will involve the neighboring Arab nations around Israel… and probably the fulfillment of the prophecy of the utter destruction of Damascus, the capital city of

Syria, as it is given in Isaiah 17.

    b. The other war is the Gog of Magog War described in Ezek. 38-39 which will be a Russian-led invasion of a coalition of Islamic nations into Israel.

In both of these wars, Israel will come out the victor. So, these wars will be **hardships followed by a blessing**. And, current events in the Middle East and with Russia are definitely setting the stage ***now*** for them to happen.

So, **Point 1** is that if we base our conclusion on what happened in the last three Feast Day Tetrads, then **this** Feast Day Tetrad is NOT *directly* related to the Rapture, but more likely has to do with some hardship on Israel… most likely another war. But whatever it is, it will lead to a blessing.

2. I am often asked… "In real numbers, how many years do you think we are from the Rapture of the Church, the Tribulation, and the Second Coming?"

Of course, I can't put an exact number of years on any of that. BUT, I do preach all the time about how the signs of our day tell us unequivocally that we are living in the end times… the last days of the Church Age. That is, we are definitely in the SEASON of our Lord's return.

SO… **IF** this Feast Day Tetrad is associated with the Psalm 83 War or the Magog War, since these wars will happen in the LAST DAYS, this would stand as another confirmation that we are now living in the Last Days. But we will just have to wait and see.

Likewise, if ***this*** Feast Day Tetrad is NOT associated with one of these last days wars, it is very unlikely that another Feast Day Tetrad will be associated with them because there won't be another Feast Day Tetrad THIS CENTURY! And to be perfectly honest, I just can't believe that our Lord's coming is over a century away. There are too many other signs being fulfilled today for it to be that far into the future.

So even though this Feast Day Tetrad does not *__directly__* point to the Rapture of the Church, if it coincides with one of these Last Days Wars, then it would definitely mean that we're living at the end of the Church Age… which means, of course, that the Rapture is at hand! It could prove to be another phenomenon of the last days, and therefore, in an *__indirect__* way, be another indicator that the Rapture is near.

Solar Eclipses

Our discussion so far has been on the lunar eclipses of the moon. But the Scriptures also say **that the sun will be darkened**. So, we need to look at the possibility that that is a reference to solar eclipses.

Remember that Jewish tradition holds that just as lunar eclipses are associated with events related to the Jews, they also believe that solar eclipses relate to events in the Gentile nations.

It just so happens that there will be two solar eclipses in the year 2015. One is a partial eclipse, but the other is a total eclipse and *__both of them fall on significant Jewish dates.__*

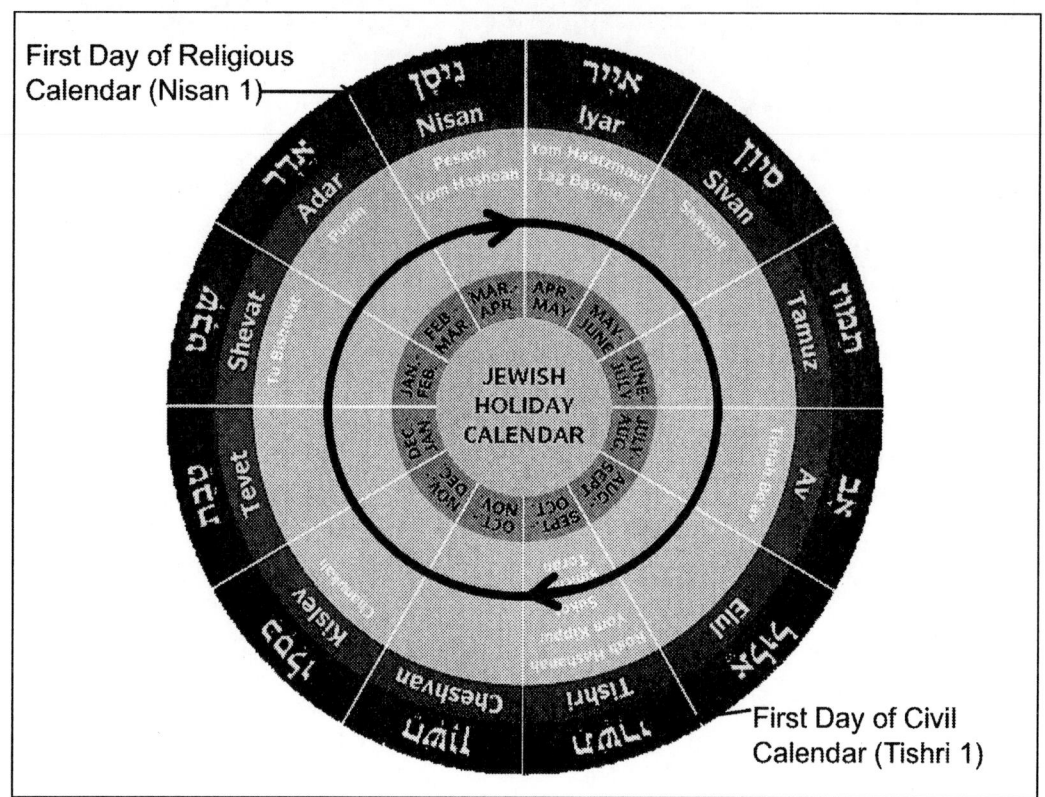

The Jews have two calendars... a RELIGIOUS calendar, and a CIVIL calendar. Actually, they are the same calendar with the same twelve months. But they START at opposite times of the 12-month cycle. The religious calendar starts on Nisan 1 and the civil calendar starts six months later on Tishri 1 (New Year's Day).

Of the two solar eclipses that will happen in 2015, the first one (the full solar eclipse), will happen on Nisan 1, the first day of the religious calendar. The second one (the partial solar eclipse) will happen six months later on Tishri 1, the first day of the civil calendar... the exact OPPOSITE days on the Jewish calendar system.

I wonder if there will be some significant historical event that will happen on those two days that is related to the Gentile nations.

Oh! Tishri 1, the first day of the civil calendar (or, the first day of the seventh month on the religious calendar)... just happens to also be the day of the Feast of Trumpets! On our Gregorian calendar, that will be Sept. 13, 2015.

So, look at what's going to happen in 2014 and 2015:

In 2014...
Nisan 14 (April 15) (Passover) - Total lunar eclipse (blood red moon)
Tishri 15 (Oct. 8) (Tabernacles) - Total lunar eclipse (blood red moon)
In 2015...
Nisan 1 (March 24) (Beginning of the religious year) – Total solar eclipse
Nisan 14 (April 4) (Passover) - Total lunar eclipse (blood red moon)
Tishri 1 (Sept. 14) (Beginning of the civil year, Trumpets) – Partial solar eclipse
Tishri 15 (Sept. 28) (Tabernacles) - Total lunar eclipse (blood red moon)

Certainly 2014 and 2015 should prove to be very interesting!

- It's hard to say that having four consecutive blood red moons falling exactly on the dates of the first and the last of the Seven Annual Feasts of Israel in two consecutive years, **is just coincidental.**

- It's hard to say that in that same time frame, there will be two solar eclipses that will fall exactly on the first day of the religious calendar and the first day of the civil calendar... which ALSO happens to be the day of the Feast of Trumpets... **is just coincidental.**

But listen! There's even MORE to this!

Seven Year Sabbatical Cycle

God established for the Jews a law called **The Sabbatical Year Cycle.** You will remember that before the children of Israel went into the Promise Land, God said,

Lev 25:2 - *"Speak unto the children of Israel, and say unto them, When ye come into the land which I give you, then shall the land keep a sabbath unto the LORD.*
3   Six years thou shalt sow thy field, and six years thou shalt prune thy vineyard, and gather in the fruit thereof;
4   But in the seventh year shall be a sabbath of rest unto the land, a sabbath for the LORD: thou shalt neither sow thy field, nor prune thy vineyard."

So, for six years, the Israelites could plant their land and harvest their crops. But on the seventh year, they were not to till the soil... or plant or cultivate anything... or harvest any crop. In fact, if anything grew up "freewill", so to speak, they were to leave it in the field. That seventh year was a very special sabbatical year called a "Sabbath for the Lord" (in Hebrew = "shmitah")

According to the Jewish calendar, those seven-year cycles are still recognized. I don't know that they are strictly observed by the people in Israel today, but they are still designated on the calendar.

Presently, we are in the Jewish *__Civil Calendar__* year 5774 (2014), which started on Sept. 5, 2013 and will end on Sept. 24, 2014. [1] This is year SIX in the seven year cycle.

Next year (5775 on the Jewish calendar) which starts on Sept. 25, 2014 and ends Sept. 13, 2015, **_will be the sabbatical year_** ("shmitah", seventh year of the seven-year cycle). [2]

So, starting on Sept. 25, 2014 and going to Sept. 13, 2015 will be the "Shmitah" (Sabbatical Year).

[For the reason the sabbatical year is based on the civil calendar, starting in the fall, see http://www.itsaboutthattime.net/year_begins_fall.htm]

CONCLUSION:

(1) The seven annual feasts of Israel were established by God to force the Jews to remember great events in which He blessed them (Example – Passover = the deliverance from Egypt).

(2) But, Jesus has been and will become the living fulfillment of each feast.
He literally fulfilled the first four feasts:

- He died on Passover.
- He was buried on Unleavened Bread.
- He was resurrected on Firstfruits.
- He sent the Holy Spirit to the Church on Pentecost.

If He literally fulfilled the first four feasts, then we can expect Him to literally fulfill the last three of the feasts.

(3) We do not know HOW He's going to fulfill the last three feasts. But it's **_possible_** that He may fulfill the Feast of

(4) The Bible clearly associates the "darkening of the sun and the blood red moon" with the days immediately preceding the Second Coming. These may be references to solar and lunar eclipses.

(5) In the years 2014-2015, the very unusual "Feast Day Tetrad" will occur with four consecutive blood red moons happening on the feast days of Passover and Tabernacles... the only time this will happen this century.

(6) Likewise, two solar eclipses will occur in 2015... one on the first day of the religious calendar and the other on the first day of the civil calendar. This second one will happen on the day of the Feast of Trumpets.

(7) In the years 2014-2015, the next Jewish **_sabbatical year_** will occur.

Trumpets by rapturing the Church since the Rapture will include the blowing of the heavenly trumpets.

One Final Word:

I do not know, nor does anyone else know the exact time that our Lord Jesus is going to come and rapture His Church! These lessons on the Feasts of Israel and the coming unusual occurrences of eclipses and how they may relate to Bible Prophecy is NOT positive proof for any date for the Rapture of the Church. However, it may be viewed as another indicator of the nearness of our Lord's coming. Though we may not know the exact time of His coming, there are many signs happening in our time that point to the fact that we are certainly in the "season" of it. This Feast Day Tetrad may just be another one of these many signs. But we will have to wait until it's passed to know this for sure.

But when all of the signs of our day are taken together, then we must certainly heed our Lord's words in

Luke 21:28 - *"And when these things begin to come to pass, then look up, and lift up your heads; **for your redemption draweth nigh**."*

----

(1) http://www.hebcal.com/holidays/2015-2016
(2) http://www.chabad.org/library/article_cdo/aid/562077/jewish/Shemitah-101.htm
(3) http://eclipse.gsfc.nasa.gov/LEcat5/LE2001-2100.html

Lesson 1 Quiz

1. For the seven annual feasts that God told the Israelites to observe, it would require the men to make a pilgrimage to the Tabernacle (or Temple) _____ times per year.

2. According to Matt. 5:17, Jesus said He did not come to destroy the law, but to _____ it.

3. Jesus has been the living fulfillment of the first four feasts. What is the name of the next feast that He will fulfill?

4. He MAY fulfill the next feast with the _____ of the Church.

5. T or F   By understanding the Feasts of Israel, we can know the day that Jesus will rapture His Church.

6. The Scriptures referring to the darkening of the light of the sun and of the moon MIGHT be a reference to the natural occurrence of _____.

7. Joel 2:31 - "*The sun shall be turned into darkness, and the moon into blood, _____ the great and the terrible day of the LORD come.*"

8. There are two kinds of eclipses. What are they?

9. A "Blood Red Moon" eclipse is actually a total _____ eclipse.

10. Four "Blood Red Moons" in a row, without any partial eclipses in between is known as a _____.

11. T or F   There will be only ONE Feast Day Tetrad this century and we are in the midst of it now (2014 - 2015).

12. In the law of the Seven Year Sabbatical Cycle, the Jewish people were to observe the seventh year by doing what?

Lesson 1 Quiz Answers

1. three
2. fulfill
3. Feast of Trumpets
4. Rapture
5. False
6. Eclipses
7. before
8. Solar eclipses and Lunar eclipses
9. lunar
10. Tetrad
11. True
12. Allowing their land to lie fallow (unplanted)

Lesson 2

ISIS, Damascus, and the Prophecy of Isaiah 17

When the prophet Isaiah preached, his message was very straightforward. He basically told the people to either REPENT, or else suffer God's JUDGMENT. Unfortunately, for the most part, there was no genuine repentance, so God used the Babylonians to judge Judah, even though Isaiah did not live to see that judgment.

In chapters 13-23, the prophet goes through a list of nations who were at various times the enemies of Israel and he pronounces God judgment upon those nations. Of particular interest to us in this lesson is chapter seventeen which describes the destruction of the capital city of Syria… the city of Damascus.

Let's begin by looking at the time when Isaiah made this prophecy.

During Isaiah's time, the Assyrian Empire was expanding to the west and south and becoming the ruling regional empire of the day. So, during the reign of the Assyrian King Tiglath-Pileser III, both Damascus and the northern kingdom of Israel (the ten tribes) were subdued and forced to pay taxes to Assyria.

So, in 734 BC, King Rezin of Syria and King Pekah of Israel formed an alliance to stop paying tribute to the Assyrians. And to bolster their resistance, they went to King Ahaz of Judah and attempted to force him into their alliance against Assyria, but Ahaz refused. So, then they tried to defeat Judah, but were not successful (II Kings 16:5). So, King Rezin of Syria went to the southern port city of Eilat in Judah and took the city under Syrian control. It appears that this move convinced King Ahaz of Judah to retaliate against Syria and Israel by taking the Temple treasures along with his own silver and gold and sending it as a gift to Tiglath-Pileser III of Assyria and asking him to attack Israel and Syria (II Kings 16:7-8), which he did. First, the Assyrians came down took the Syrian capital of Damascus…

II Kings 16:9 - *"And the king of Assyria hearkened unto him* [Ahaz]: *for the king of Assyria went up against Damascus, and took it, and carried the people of it captive to Kir, and slew Rezin."*

Then, he went on to capture most of Israel. About ten years later, when Hoshea was the king of what was left of Israel, he tried to make an alliance with Egypt against Assyria who at that time was ruled by King Shalmaneser V. So, Shalmaneser returned to Israel and captured the capital city of Samaria in 722 BC. This was the end of the kingdom of the northern ten tribes of Israel.

Now, I give you that short history lesson on the destruction of Israel and the city of Damascus in Syria because some scholars point to that as the fulfillment of the judgment of destruction that Isaiah prophesied in chapter 17. But is it? Well, let's look at it.

I'll begin by giving three arguments why the Assyrian invasion was the fulfillment of Isaiah 17 and then I'll present three arguments why its fulfillment is still futuristic.

Three reasons why Isa. 17 WAS fulfilled by the Assyrian destruction in the 8th century BC:

(1) We see that judgments against both Damascus and Israel are mentioned in this one chapter. It speaks of Damascus as being destroyed and Israel as being severely beaten down. It is as if these

two countries are in some way tied together in this prophecy.

Well, as we noted in the historical account, Syria and Israel had allied themselves together against Judah and the Assyrian empire. And when the Assyrians retaliated against this rebellion, Damascus was first defeated by the Assyrians. Then, immediately after that, a large part of Israel was also defeated leaving it stripped of its former glory. So, it makes sense that God's prophetic judgment against Damascus would be tied to His judgment against Israel.

(2) Verses 5-6 speak using the analogy of harvesting corn, grapes, and olives as a picture of how Israel will be stripped like the harvest of produce from the field.

Vs. 5 says it will be like when the harvestman pulls the ears of corn in the valley of Rephaim between Jerusalem and Bethlehem that supposedly produced beautiful stands of corn. So, the idea is that the harvestman in Rephaim would attempt to gather every single ear of that beautiful corn. Hence, the enemies of Israel would attempt to "gather out" every single person.

But verse 6 begins with the word "Yet"...

Isa 17:6 – *__Yet__ gleaning grapes shall be left in it, as the shaking of an olive tree, two or three berries in the top of the uppermost bough, four or five in the outmost fruitful branches thereof, saith the LORD God of Israel.*

In other words, even though the invading forces will attempt to take every single person, a few people will be left behind like the "gleaning grapes" left on the vine or the two or three olives left in the uppermost limb of the tree.

It was standard foreign policy of the Assyrians, when they defeated a people, to deport most of them from their homeland, leaving only the poorest of the citizens there (like the few "gleaning grapes" or uppermost olives left behind). Then, they would bring in Assyrian people to interbreed with the remaining population in an attempt to completely erase the heritage of that defeated country.

Well, that is exactly what happened when the Assyrians defeated Israel. They deported most of the Israelis and imported some Assyrians to live among those Jews left behind. This mixed race of Jews and Assyrians became a race of cross-breeds called the Samaritans whom the Jews hated so much later on when Jesus was in Judea.

(3) Verses 12-14 speak of the judgment that God will bring down upon the nation that destroys Israel.

Isa 17:13b - *...God shall rebuke them, and they shall flee far off, and shall be chased as the chaff of the mountains before the wind, and like a rolling thing before the whirlwind.*
14 And behold at eveningtide trouble; and before the morning he is not. This is the portion of them that spoil us, and the lot of them that rob us.

My paraphrase of that verse would go like this…
God will rebuke them and they will flee before their enemies like chaff flying in the mountain wind, or like a tumbleweed rolling in front of a whirlwind.
Their destruction will be quick. They'll have trouble in the evening and by morning they will not exist. This is what will befall those who spoil us (Israel) and rob us.

Well, is that what happened to the Assyrians? They were eventually also destroyed... by the Babylonians. Get this. God used the Assyrians to destroy sinful Israel. Then, He used the Babylonians to destroy the sinful Assyrians... who even though they repented for a short time under the preaching of Jonah, soon turned back to their idolatrous ways. After that, God used the Medes and Persians to destroy the sinful Babylonians.

The point is this...
God can use one sinner to judge another, and then judge the sinner He just used!

So, it looks like the pronounced judgment of vss. 12-14 on the ones who would destroy Israel is a perfect picture of what happened to the Assyrians.

Well, that's three good arguments for the ***historical fulfillment***of Isaiah 17 when Israel and Damascus were both conquered by the Assyrians. And I'm sure there are a number of other points that could be made to say that this chapter was fulfilled in the 8th century BC.

But wait a minute...
There may also be some reasons to believe in a ***future fulfillment*** of this prophecy. Let me give you now three good reasons why this prophecy will likely be fulfilled in the future:

(1) The first point I would make in the argument for a future fulfillment is found in verse 1.

Isa 17:1 - *The burden of Damascus. Behold, Damascus is taken away from being a city, and it shall be a ruinous heap.*

The description given to the destruction of Damascus seems to be much more severe than the defeat she suffered at the hands of the Assyrians. It clearly says that the city of Damascus will suffer such destruction that it will no longer be a city, but will only exist as a "ruinous heap"... a pile of rubble.

Did the Assyrians accomplish such total destruction of Damascus?

The Wikipedia Encyclopedia says this about the city of Damascus:

"Excavations at Tell Ramad on the outskirts of the city have demonstrated that Damascus has been inhabited as early as 8000 to 10,000 BC. It is due to this that Damascus is considered to be the oldest continually inhabited city in the world."

Historically, Damascus has been conquered many times, but it has never been utterly destroyed. It has been, as the encyclopedia points out, continually inhabited for thousands of years.

If we look back at the Scriptural account of Tiglath-Pileser III's taking of Damascus again, it says in

II Kings 16:9 - *"And the king of Assyria hearkened unto him [Ahaz]: for the king of Assyria went up against Damascus, and **took it**, and carried the people of it captive to Kir, and slew Rezin."*

It doesn't say he ***destroyed*** the city... or, that he made it into a ruinous heap. It says he **"took it"** (in the KJV).

This same wording ("took it") is used in:

- New King James Version
- The Revised Standard Version
- The American Standard Version
- The Darby Translation
- The Webster Version
- And, The Hebrew Names Version

The New International Version and the New American Standard use the words "captured it". And the Young Literal Translation says they "seized it"

But none of these translations indicate that he DESTROYED it or in any way left it as a heap of rubble.

The Strong's Concordance defines the word translated here as "took" as "to seize" or "chiefly to capture". So, again, the Biblical description of the Assyrian defeat of Damascus does not indicate that the city was destroyed… but only that it was captured and its citizens deported.

So, that means that the fulfillment of this prophecy is still to come at some point in the future when the city will be completely destroyed. There is coming a day when Damascus will be reduced to a "ruinous heap".

(2) Along those same lines of thought, verse 2 says

Isa 17:2 -   *"The cities of Aroer are forsaken: they shall be for flocks, which shall lie down, and none shall make them afraid."*

The idea here is that the cities of Aroer are completely void of human life. I want you to notice that there is no indication that the buildings of these cities will be reduced to rubble as it says about Damascus in verse one. It just says that the cities are "forsaken" and that those cities will be for flocks (sheep or goats) that will come in and lay down and there will be no one to shoo them away.

Get this picture… whole cities with empty buildings… no people, just empty buildings where wild goats wander in and out. The New Living Translation says it this way:
"The cities of Aroer will be deserted. Sheep will graze in the streets and lie down unafraid. There will be no one to chase them away."

But where are the cities of Aroer?

There were three cities in ancient times called "Aroer"… two of them east of the Jordan River. One of those was in the territory of Gad, east of the half way point of the Jordan River and the other one east of the Dead Sea on the Arnon River. Both of these seem to be too far south of Damascus to be associated with its destruction.

The Jewish Encyclopedia claims that this phrase "cities of Aroer" is a mistranslation and should be rendered simply "the cities thereof" speaking of the cities around Damascus. In Isaiah's time, it was the Aramaeans who lived in and around Damascus, and thus the cities of Aroer, they say, is just a reference to the Aramaean territory surrounding Damascus. The area of Aram would include modern day Syria and southern Lebanon.

Again, historically, there has never been an occasion where all the towns and villages and cities in that area have ALL been void of human life.

(3) In verses 4-6, as we mentioned earlier, we have a description of Israel being (not destroyed altogether), but seriously hurt and wasted. Vs. 4 says *"the glory of Jacob [Israel] shall be made thin, and the fatness of his flesh shall wax lean."*

Then, it goes on to say in verse 7, *"At that day shall a man look to his Maker, and his eyes shall have respect to the Holy One of Israel."*
In other words, when Damascus is destroyed…
And the cities of Aroer are made void of human life…
And Israel is decimated…
Then, men will turn to the God of Israel.

But WHAT men was he talking about?
Vs. 8 goes on to say that "he" (those same men) will not look for solace in their man-made altars, or in their places of the idolatrous worship (groves and images)…

Vs. 9 says that in that day "his" strong cities will be forsaken… (talking about those same men)

Now, look at vs. 10
10 *"Because thou hast forgotten the God of thy salvation, …"*
WHO is it that will suffer because they have forgotten the God of their salvation? The people of Israel!

So, back in vs. 7, it is the men of Israel who will look to their maker and have respect to the God of Israel. In other words, those Israelis who survive this devastation will cry out to God in repentance.

Now, there's not much doubt that whatever Israelis managed to escape the death of the Assyrians, probably did look to the true God of Israel for help. This would be a natural thing for them to do. But we don't have any record of a sweeping revival coming over that remnant that remained after the Assyrian invasion.

The point is this…
If Israel as a nation turns to the true God of the universe because of some devastation that she suffers, it hasn't happened yet. Even today she is living in unbelief and disobedience. So, this must be a reference to some future turning to God.

So, there you have it. I've made three reasonably good arguments as to why Isaiah 17 was fulfilled **historically** in the Assyrian invasion of Damascus and Israel. And, I've made three reasonably good arguments as to why Isaiah 17 will be fulfilled at some point **in the future.**

So which is it? Has it been fulfilled? Or, Will it be fulfilled?
I believe the best answer is BOTH.

There are many OT prophecies that have had some PRE-fulfillment in history, but are still waiting for complete fulfillment at some future date.

An example of this can be found in the book of Daniel. Daniel 7 and 8 both speak of a certain person symbolically as "a little horn", but they are two different people. The little horn of chap. 7 is a reference to Antichrist, the man of sin who is to come. But the little horn of chap. 8 is a reference to Antiochus Epiphanes, a notoriously evil despot that persecuted the Jews in the 2nd century BC.

God gives us a clear picture of what the coming Antichrist is going to be like by pointing us to Antiochus. If we want to know what kind of man Antichrist will be… how he will operate… etc., all we have to do is look at Antiochus.

Daniel 11 tells us about Antiochus in verses 21-35, but starting in verse 36, the king that does according to his will and exalts himself and magnifies himself is speaking of Antichrist. In these Scriptures, Antiochus is a PRE-fulfillment of the FINAL fulfillment that will come in the person of Antichrist.

Likewise, the Assyrian invasion of Damascus and Israel is a PRE-fulfillment of what will be the FINAL fulfillment at some future date when Damascus is reduced to a pile of rubble.

There is no doubt that both Damascus (Syria) and the northern kingdom of Israel suffered terribly at the hands of the Assyrians around 730 BC. But, (at least in the case of Damascus) life continued. The city continued… and it DOES continue to this day! So the final and complete fulfillment will come at some point in the future when Damascus will be utterly destroyed… when it will no longer be a city, but will become just a pile of rubble (or, as the KJV says, a "ruinous heap").

Let me show you one more interesting little note that points to a dual fulfillment of this prophecy:

Notice in verse 3, that Israel is referred to as Ephraim, the largest of the ten tribes of the northern kingdom. It is just as the southern kingdom which was made up of Judah and Benjamin is often called "Judah" in the Bible. So this is a clear reference to the destruction of the northern kingdom… which happened in 722 BC.

But in verse 4, it says that the "glory of **Jacob** shall be made thin". Now, again, the name of Jacob was often used to refer to the northern kingdom. But Jacob was, of course, the father of all 12 tribes of Israel… and his name was changed by God to Israel. In many places in the Bible, the name of Jacob is synonymously used to refer to the whole nation of Israel… the whole 12 tribes (Psa. 79:7, 85:1, 99:4, Isa. 2:5, 6, 9:8, 14:1, etc.)

So, in verse 3, we have a clear reference to the ten tribes of the northern kingdom. But in verse 4, we have a reference that could apply to all the tribes of Israel, or **even to the modern day nation** of Israel. Is that significant? Well, it is certainly worth our noting it.

Now, if we can accept this (the idea of a dual fulfillment)… If we believe that there is still some future, complete fulfillment of this prophecy… let's look at what this whole chapter says about the future of Damascus and Israel.

In summary of the chapter, we could break it down this way:

Vs. 1 – Damascus will be reduced to a pile of rubble and will no longer be a city.
Vs. 2 – The surrounding cities will become void of human life, even though their buildings will still be standing.
Vs. 3 – Neither Israel or Syria will any longer be a "fortress" (stronghold, fortified city).
Vs. 4-6 – Israel will be greatly decimated, but not destroyed. A remnant (like the "gleaning grapes" of the harvest) will be left.
Vs. 7-11 – Israel will then look to the true God of Israel. This will happen in that day when everything will be fine at planting time, but by harvest time, it will be a day of grief and of desperate sorrow.
Vs. 12-14 – God Himself will destroy those who have attempted to destroy Israel.

Some Bible prophecy scholars believe that the destruction of Damascus in Isaiah 17 will be a part of a regional war between Israel and her Arab neighbors [see "Isralestine" by Bill Salus [1]]. This is often referred to as the Psalm 83 War in which the IDF (Israeli Defense Forces) will decimate those Arab nations around Israel. It is thought that an alliance of these Middle Eastern Muslim Arab nations will attack Israel, but will suffer utter defeat by Israel and the borders of Israel will be expanded to include those nations. In the process of this war, Israel will destroy Damascus in fulfillment of Isaiah 17.

Space won't allow us to investigate the prophecy of the Psalm 83 War here. However, suffice it to say that this author certainly recognizes it as a strong possibility and that ***should*** it happen, Isaiah 17 will most likely be a part of that war.

Our next question is this:
If there is a FUTURE fulfillment of this prophecy, are we seeing any movement in that direction today?

ISIS or ISIL or IS?

A hot topic in the news right now is the Islamic terrorist group called ISIS (Islamic State of Iraq and Syria) that is militarily taking over the nation of Iraq. After the United States expenditure of some $845 billion [2] and the loss of 4486 US lives [3] to free that country from the death grip of "the Butcher of Bagdad", Saddam Hussein, and other terrorist groups like Al Qaeda, it is most disheartening to see Iraq being overrun by yet another Islamic terrorist group that will remove whatever has been accomplished in establishing a free democracy there. The media reports say that ISIS has taken most of the cities in northern Iraq and have moved to within just a few miles of the capital city of Bagdad. It seems that the Iraqi army is helpless in defending its people from this aggression and aside from some outside military intervention, the fall of the Iraqi government to ISIS is imminent.

But exactly who is this "ISIS"? Where do they come from and what is their goal? Where do they get their financial support? And, are they a threat to the peace and security of other countries? And most importantly, is what they are doing going to play into the fulfillment of Bible prophecy in some way? To answer these questions, we must start with a review of the current civil war that is taking place in Syria.

Syrian Civil War
In 1963, a "state of emergency" was put in place by the Syrian government that essentially suspended all civil rights and gave the president dictatorial powers. That "state of emergency" remains in effect until today. As the Syrian Defense Minister in 1970, **Hafez al-Assad** seized control of the government and appointed himself as the undisputed leader. He ruled Syria as a strong-fisted dictator for some thirty years until his death in 2000, at which time he was succeeded by his son, **Bashar al-Assad**, who is still the president.

In January, 2011, protests broke out calling for political reform and the re-instatement of civil rights. But Assad, following in the footsteps of his father, responded to the protests with military strength, killing many of the protesters. This initial bloodshed created an uprising bent on overthrowing the Assad regime. To date, the Syrian Civil War, now in its fourth year, has resulted in an estimated death toll of over 150,000 citizens. [4]

About 74% of the Syrian population is Sunni Muslim and 13% is Shi'a Muslim. [5] Assad and the ruling leaders are Alawites, a sect of

Shi'a Islam. So the deep running hatred between the Sunni populace and Shi'a leadership is rooted in centuries old theology differences within the Islamic religion.

Others in the region are also divided along these same religious lines. **Iran**, which is about 98% Shi'a has been a strong supporter of the Assad government. Likewise, the **Hezbollah** terrorists in the southern part of the bordering nation of Lebanon is a Shi'a terrorist group that receives its financial and weapons support from the Syrian and Iranian governments. So they have joined forces with the Syrian government of Bashar al-Assad.

Iraq is about 65% Shi'a and 35% Sunni, but it has been the Sunnis who have controlled the government since the days of Saddam Hussein who was Sunni. The supposedly secular, democratic government left in place after the US troop withdrawal in 2011 has proven to be more sectarian under the leadership of Shi'a Muslim **Prime Minister Nouri al-Maliki** with accusations that most of the government leadership positions have been given to Shi'as. Also, Sunnis in northern Iraq claim that they have been abused by government forces and have thus given allegiance to the ISIS Sunnis.

So the defining factor as to whether a group is in support of Bashar al-Assad and his Syrian government or in support of the Syrian opposition forces, is whether they are Sunni or Shi'a Muslims. The Shi'as (Iran, Hezbollah in Lebanon, and the Iraqi government) are in support of Bashar al-Assad. The Sunnis (northern Iraqi citizens and ISIS) are in support of the Syrian rebels.

Now, among the rebel forces in Syria, there are many independent groups fighting against the government in various parts of the country and even against one another. Initially, however, many of the defecting Syrian army officers formed a group called the **Free Syrian**

Army that was able to integrate a number of the rebel factions and work in conjunction with the **Syrian National Council**, a Turkey based opposition coalition of various councils and groups working to overthrow the Assad regime. But the many identities and beliefs of those who fall in the "opposition camp" are very diverse and they mostly work independently of one another.

However, the host of rebel groups fighting against the Assad government can be separated into two divisions…
(1) the moderate seculars like the Free Syrian Army who want a government that represents all sectarian groups equally, and
(2) the Islamist, al-Quaeda linked groups like **Jabhat al-Nusra** who are striving to establish an Islamic, Sharia law based government.

Not only are these two sides fighting against the Syrian government, but quite often violence breaks out between them and even among factions within their ranks. So, anarchy reigns in Syria with widespread violence, torture, and bloodshed. Millions of refugees have fled the country in search of some sense of safety.

Now, among the Islamist groups fighting in Syria, there has arisen **ISIS**, a brutally cruel al-Quaeda splinter group that feels no compunction about massacring those it views as its enemies. ISIS stands for the **"Islamic State of Iraq and Syria"**, but it is increasingly being called **ISIL** which stands for the **"Islamic State of Iraq and the Levant"** because the word "Levant" includes all the nations at the eastern end of the Mediterranean Sea (Syria, Lebanon, Israel, Jordan, Cypress, Egypt, Turkey and Iraq). Officially, however, it is now calling itself **IS** which stands for the **"Islamic State"**, which is their ultimate goal… to be known as THE Islamic caliphate for all Muslims. It is easy to see even from these name changes that the aspirations of ISIS is to become the Islamic caliphate, i.e., one religious/political state to rule over all Muslims.

It is reported that their main financial support has come from within the territories that they control with only about 5% coming from outside donors who are sympathetic to their cause. [6] Within the cells of their occupied territory, extortion and bank robbery have been the primary methods for their funding with a reported $429 million US and quantities of gold bullion stolen from the central bank of Mosul, a city in northern Iraq. Also, they have generated millions of dollars in capital from oil fields they've captured in eastern Syria. According to Iraqi intelligence officers, an ISIS operative revealed a stash of computer flash drives that detailed the ISIS financial assets. The total worth of those assets is over $2 billion, making it the richest jihadist group in the world. [7]

Along with those finances, there have been millions of dollars worth of military equipment captured from the Iraqi army, most of it US made. This includes night vision goggles, many different military rifles including large machine guns, grenade launchers, surface-to-air Stinger missiles, Humvees, T-55 and T-72 tanks, M198 Howitzer artillery, anti-aircraft guns, and some UH-60 Blackhawk helicopters and some cargo planes. [8] With this kind of weaponry in its possession and having the wealth that it does and by having a very organized chain of command, ISIS has moved from being a disjointed terrorist group to become a military militia to now an organized conventional army. Not only are they the most brutal jihadist group we've ever seen, but they are also the richest, and most well equipped one we've ever seen.

In just a few days' time, ISIS moved from its locations in eastern Syria and captured a major portion of northern Iraq (including the cities of Mosul and Tikrit) where they found Sunni tribal leaders who felt oppressed by the mostly Shi'a Iraqi government and were ready to join forces with them against their own nation. The regular Iraqi army, for the most part, either retreated or changed into civilian clothes and deserted.

Now, reports are indicating ISIS may move next to the adjoining nation of Jordan where they already have some well established cell groups. The mostly Sunni population of Jordan is not in strong support of their King Abdullah and it is felt that they (like the Sunnis in northern Iraq) will join the ISIS forces. If northern Jordan could be taken, then this would also give ISIS strategic ground around Syria's capital city of Damascus which is only about 100 miles north of Amman. [9]

On Sept. 10, 2014, President Obama announced that he is authorizing an all-out air campaign by the United States Air Force on ISIS. Up to that time, the US had only made limited air strikes on them. He stated that it is our goal to destroy ISIS completely. However, most military analysts agree that it will be impossible to completely destroy ISIS without using some ground troops to root them out of their hiding places. But public sentiment in the US is strongly against putting any of our soldiers there, so it raises doubt as to whether this air campaign alone will get rid of ISIS.

Therefore, at this point it is unclear whether ISIS will continue its aggression and further spread its borders, or if the US (along with those who may help) will eradicate the terrorist group and reduce it to another name that once played a part in history.

But, whichever way it goes, we could certainly see an escalation in the near term. God forbid, but ISIS could make a 9/11/01 type terrorist attack in the US in retaliation. That would raise the ire of the American people that could lead to the use of US ground forces against ISIS… thus, an all-out war. On the other hand, if ISIS is not destroyed, they will undoubtedly continue their expansion towards

Israel where they will meet a very powerful military that can destroy them. In either scenario, it is easy to see how a regional war in the Middle East is on the horizon.

So, will ISIS play a part in the fulfillment of Bible prophecy? That is something that only God knows the answer to. However, a regional war could develop into the Psalm 83 War and/or the fulfillment of the Isaiah 17 prophecy of the destruction of Damascus.

There are three things that ISIS needs to remember:

(1) *"Behold, he that keepeth Israel shall neither slumber nor sleep."* (Psalm 121:3)

(2) God declares that… *"In that day will I make the governors of Judah like an hearth of fire among the wood, and like a torch of fire in a sheaf; and they shall devour all the people round about, on the right hand and on the left…*

*In that day shall the L*ORD *defend the inhabitants of Jerusalem; and he that is feeble among them at that day shall be as David; and the house of David shall be as God, as the angel of the L*ORD *before them."* (Zech. 12:6a, 8)

And God says…

(3) *"The burden of Damascus* [is this:] *Damascus is taken away from being a city, and it shall be a ruinous heap."* (Isaiah 17:1)

----

(1) Bill Salus, "Isralestine, The Ancient Blueprints of the Future Middle East" (HighWay, Crane, MO: 2008)
(2) http://en.wikipedia.org/wiki/Iraq_War#Financial_cost
(3) http://en.wikipedia.org/wiki/Casualties_of_the_Iraq_War
(4) http://www.reuters.com/article/2014/04/01/us-syria-crisis-toll-idUSBREA300YX20140401
(5) http://en.wikipedia.org/wiki/Islam_in_Syria
(6) http://en.wikipedia.org/wiki/Islamic_State_of_Iraq_and_the_Levant#

(7) http://www.theguardian.com/world/2014/jun/15/iraq-isis-arrest-jihadists-wealth-power
(8) http://en.wikipedia.org/wiki/Islamic_State_of_Iraq_and_the_Levant#Equipment
(9) http://www.wallstreetdaily.com/2014/07/03/isis-declares-caliphate/

Lesson 2 Quiz

1. The prophecy of Isaiah 17 is about the destruction of the city of _____ which is the capital of _____.

2. In the year _____, the capital city of _____ in the northern kingdom of Israel was destroyed by the _____ empire.

3. Isaiah 17:12-14 speak of the destruction that God will bring upon the nation who destroys Israel. This was fulfilled when the Assyrian Empire was conquered by the _____ empire.

4. The first argument that is usually made in favor of a FUTURE fulfillment of Isaiah 17 is that the city of _____ has never been completely destroyed as described in Isaiah 17:1.

5. T or F   The towns and villages of Aroer have never been void of human life.

6. Some Bible prophecy scholars believe that fulfillment of the Isaiah 17 prophecy will take place during a regional war between Israel and her Arab neighbors called the _____ War.

7. ISIS stands for _____ _____ __ _____ and _____.

8. The current president (July, 2014) of Syria is _____ _____.

9. As of today (July, 2014) it is estimated that over _____ citizens of Syria have died in the civil war that is going on there.

10. Iraq has a majority of _____ Muslims, but the current administration is mostly _____ Muslims.

11. T or F   ISIS believes in a secular, non-religious government.

12. T or F   We know that ISIS will definitely play a part in the fulfillment of Isaiah 17.

Lesson 2 Quiz Answers

1. Damascus, Syria

2. 722 BC, Samaria, Assyrian

3. Babylonian

4. Damascus

5. True

6. Psalm 83

7. Islamic State of Iraq and Syria

8. Bashar al-Assad

9. lunar

10. Sunni, Shi'a

11. False. They want to establish an Islamic government based on Sharia law.

12. False. Only God knows how stage will be set to fulfill Isa. 17. However, it is POSSIBLE that ISIS could instigate the Psalm 83 War and thus, the fulfillment of Isaiah 17.

Lesson 3

The War of Gog of Magog – Part 1
Ezekiel 38-39
(Footnotes for this lesson are at the end of Lesson 5)

Ezek 38:1-2 – *And the word of the LORD came unto me, saying,*

2 Son of man, set thy face against Gog, the land of Magog, the chief prince of Meshech and Tubal, and prophesy against him,"

Ezek. 38&39 contain one of the most amazing prophecies found in the Bible. It describes an attempted attack on Israel by a coalition of nations in which God will intervene and utterly destroy the attackers on the mountains of Israel. Even though this was written over 2500 years ago, as we will see, God supplies us with a lot of details about this about this war, including:

- WHO will make the attack,
- WHAT is going to be the outcome,
- WHERE it will happen,
- WHY the attack is made, and
- To some degree… WHEN it will happen,
- The Bible even gives a description of the clean-up afterwards.

As we study this prophecy, we will look at these various aspects that God details for us and we will also look at some RECENT DEVELOPMENTS that seem to be setting the stage for this war to happen soon.

First, we must understand that there has never been such an attack on Israel in the annals of history, nor such a miraculous intervention of

God, so we must assume that the literal fulfillment of this invasion is still futuristic. And, MOST amazing is that we are witnessing the geopolitical stage being set for this invasion TODAY as never before!

Who

Let's begin our study by looking at WHO will be involved in this attack because that is where Ezekiel begins. In the first 6 verses of Chap. 38, there are ten proper nouns given to identify the invaders. However, the primary player is identified right up front in vs. 2:

Ezek 38:2 – *"Son of man, set thy face against **Gog, the land of Magog**, the chief prince of Meshech and Tubal, and prophesy against him,"*

Who is this "Gog" from the land of "Magog"?
And, where in the world is Meshech, and Tubal?

It appears, by the account of most Bible scholars that "Gog" is ***not*** the proper name of an individual, but rather the **title** of a national leader in the same way that we would use the words "Pharaoh" or "Caesar". Gog is the title of the supreme national leader of the land of Magog.

John tells us in the book of Revelation that at the end of the Millennial Kingdom, Satan will deceive the nations of the world into rebelling against King Jesus Who will be reigning over the earth from His throne in Jerusalem at that time. And it says that among those rebellious nations will be **"Gog and Magog"** (Rev. 20:8). But this is obviously NOT a reference to the same Gog or people of Magog that fight the battle in Ezek. 38-39. It is a reference to another person who holds the "Magog position" over one thousand years later and the people of THAT day whom he rules over. So, "Gog" is a title of the supreme leader who rules over the people of Magog.

In order for us to discover the identity of who the people of Magog really are, we must go back to the original families that repopulated the earth in the days of Noah, after the flood.

You will remember that only Noah and his wife, and their three sons (Shem, Ham, and Japheth) and their wives were saved from the flood in the ark. So, these four couples were responsible for repopulating the entire earth after the flood.

Japheth, Noah's third son, was the father of seven sons, **four** of whom are named in Ezekiel 38 as the founders of the peoples who will be the coming invaders of Israel.

Gen 10:1-2 – *"Now these are the generations of the sons of Noah, Shem, Ham, and Japheth: and unto them were sons born after the flood.*
2 The sons of Japheth; **Gomer***, and* **Magog***, and Madai, and Javan, and* **Tubal***, and* **Meshech***, and Tiras."*

So, we see that Gomer, Magog, Tubal, and Meshech were the sons of Japheth, the grandsons of Noah.

The ancient Jewish historian Josephus identified the people of Magog as Scythians of the far North (*Antiquities I, Chapter 6, paragraph 1*). "Magog founded those that from him were named Magogites, but who are by the Greeks called Scythians."

According to the Encarta Encyclopedia…

"Scythians" was a name given by ancient Greek writers to a number of nomadic tribes of southeastern Europe and Asia. The name was used for those dwelling north of the **Black Sea**, between the **Carpathian Mountains** and the **Don River**, in what is now Moldova,

Ukraine, and western Russia or, in a much broader sense, all the nomadic tribes who inhabited the steppes eastward from what is now Hungary all the way to the mountains of Turkmenistan.

Chuck Missler, in his book **"The Magog Invasion"**, writes "The tortuous path from the horseback archery of the early Scyths to the nuclear missiles of the Russian Federation includes many centuries of turbulent history. The various descendents of **Magog terrorized the southern steppes of Russia from the Ukraine to the Great Wall of China."** [1]

Many **ancient** authorities identify the Magogites as the Scythians and the Scythians are known historically as the ancestors of the modern day Russians. But whether we would accept the word of these ancient historians and philosophers or not is immaterial because the Scriptures themselves declare clearly from where the invasion occurs.

Ezek 38:14-15 – *"Therefore, son of man, prophesy and say unto Gog, Thus saith the Lord GOD; In that day when my people of Israel dwelleth safely, shalt thou not know it?*
*15   And thou shalt come **from thy place out of the north parts**, thou, and many people with thee…"*

The "north parts" is translated in other translations as:
   "the distant north" (The New Living Translation)
   "the far north" (The New King James Version)
   "the remote parts of the north" (the New American Standard Version)
   "the uttermost parts of the north" (Revised Standard Version)

So, the idea is that Gog comes **from the extreme north** of Israel… which can be easily recognized as RUSSIA. In fact, when you draw a line due north from Jerusalem, it runs right through Moscow!

Thus, it appears then that **Magog, the grandson of Noah**, upon the dispersion of the people of the earth from Babel when their languages were confused, moved northward of the Black Sea and became the father of the Scythian hordes who were also the ancestors of the modern day Russians.

But our scripture passage also says that Gog is the chief prince of **Meshech and Tubal.** Remember, from Gen. 10:2 we found that Meshech and Tubal are brothers of Magog. And all three are the sons of Japheth and hence the grandsons of Noah.

According to the WebBible Encyclopedia, the people of Meshech *"were in all probability the Moschi, a people inhabiting the Moschian Mountains, between the Black and the Caspian Seas."* [2]

Likewise, according to the same encyclopedia, **Tubal** *"was probably the Tiberini people of the Greek historian Herodotus, a people of the Asiatic highland west of the Upper Euphrates, the southern range of the Caucasus, on the east of the Black Sea."* [3]

So, it seems that Meschech and Tubal were those people in the southern tip of modern Russia between the Black and Caspian Seas, along with perhaps today's countries of Georgia, Armenia, Azerbaijan, and eastern Turkey. Other sources also identify Meshech and Tubal as related to the ancient land of Anatolia which, for the most part, occupied the eastern and NE parts of modern day Turkey along the shores of the Black Sea.

Today, the nations just south of Russia, between the Black and Caspian Seas (Georgia, Azerbaijan, and Armenia) are all ex-Soviet nations, the leading nation of which was, of course, Russia. In other words, Gog, as the leader of Russia, would also be the "chief prince" over these nations that broke away from the Russian-led USSR in the last century.

So, without a doubt, GOG of Magog is the leader of modern day RUSSIA.

The Muslim Coalition

Now, look at the list of nations who will come with him:
Ezek. 38:5 - *"Persia, Ethiopia, and Libya with them; all of them with shield and helmet:*
6 Gomer, and all his bands; the house of Togarmah of the north quarters, and all his bands: and many people with thee."

Who are these people?
Persia – This one is easy to identify because the nation of Persia used that name for hundreds of years until 1935 when the name was changed to **Iran.** And, in recent years, strong ties have developed between Russia and Iran.

From WWII until the **Iranian Revolution of 1979**, the US had strong diplomatic relations with Iran when it was led by the "Shah". Consequently, Iran had very poor political ties with Russia. This was evident during the eight year long, horribly bloody war between Iraq and Iran (1980-88) when Russia sided with Saddam Hussein and supplied many weapons to the Iraqis which were used to kill many thousands of Iranians. But following the fall of the USSR in 1991, suddenly the commercial and diplomatic ties between Iran and Russia began to make dramatic improvements and soon, Iran was purchasing weapons from Russia. About this same time, Russia entered into agreements to help Iran build its first nuclear power plant.

In 2007, **Vladimir Putin**, the president of Russia, made the first official diplomatic visit to Iran by a Russian leader since 1943 and developed even stronger connections with Iran which was then led by the fanatical Muslim president **Mahmoud Ahmadinejad**. Although the West and the United Nations have levied many sanctions against Iran to try to stop its nuclear program, Russia has used its power in the UN Security Council to veto such actions as much as possible.

So, we've witnessed in the last three decades a complete reversal of the relations between Iran and Russia, going **from enemies to best friends**, and Vladimir Putin has played a major part in establishing these ties.

Iran is about 98% Muslim today.

Ethiopia – Also translated as "Cush" is a reference to the land south of Egypt along the Nile River in the area known as Nubia. Today, this would be the modern state of **Sudan**, which is about 99% Muslim.

Libya – Also translated as "Put", was according to Gen. 10:6 the third son of Ham and another grandson of Noah. According to Josephus, Put settled **Libya**, but the word is also often associated with "north Africa" exclusive of Cush. Therefore, it may also include the modern nations of **Algeria, Tunisia, and Morocco**, all of which are almost entirely Muslim.

In April 2008, Putin became the first Russian President to ever visit Libya. Then president of Libya, **Muammar Gaddafi**, developed strong relations with Russia until his overthrow and assassination in the Libyan Civil War in 2011. As of today, Libya is still in political upheaval, but you can be sure that Russia (Putin) is still active in acquiring some amount of control in whatever eventual government ends up there, especially since it is a nation with massive oil reserves.

Gomer (and all his bands) – Another son of Japheth, the people of Gomer are associated with the ancient Cimmerians who settled in central and western Anatolia (Turkey).

Togarmah (and all his bands) – Was the son of Gomer, and hence, the **great** grandson of Noah. Josephus wrote that the descendants of Togarmah were called the Phrygians and the borders of Phrygia varied greatly throughout history, but would be mainly in the area of modern Turkey and Armenia.

So, now let's summarize who we've identified the invaders of Ezekiel 38 to be:

1. The primary leader of the invasion… **Gog** (from the land of Magog, chief prince of Meshech and Tubal) - **Russia**

2. But along with Russia, we said that the Scythians ranged from east of Hungary to as far east as the Turkmenistan Mountains. So, it is possible that it may include the ex-soviet block nations of *Central Asia*… Why??? Because those nations (Kazakhstan, Uzbekistan, etc.) are more than 50% Muslim! There are over 60 million Muslims in these central Asian countries. And (as we know) Muslims hate Israel!

> **These central asian Muslim nations are:**
> **Kazakhstan**
> **Kyrgyzstan**
> **Tajikistan**
> **Uzbekistan**
> **Turkmenistan**

It's hard to say for sure that all of these nations will join with Russia, but it is likely that at least some of them will since (1) they're all Muslim nations, and (2) they are all break away nations from the old Soviet Union, of which, of course, Russia was the "mother land".

3. Meshech and Tubal – **Turkey**

4. Persia – **Iran**

5. Ethiopia – **Sudan**

6. Libya – **Libya (and most likely Algeria, Tunisia, and Morocco)**

7. Gomer and Togarmah (and all their bands) – **Turkey, Armenia**

As you can see, this is a ***huge*** coalition of nations that will come against Israel. But remember, God says in 38:23 that He will use this to magnify Himself and that He *"will be known in the eyes of many nations, and they shall know that I am the Lord."*

This is going to be such an overwhelming victory against such unbelievable odds, that the whole world is going to sit up and take notice. Many nations of the world will recognize that God Almighty has intervened miraculously to save Israel.

What God Is Going To Do

Such a massive Russian-Islamic horde has never been seen before on planet earth. The Arab wars against Israel in 1948, 1967, and 1973 will pale in comparison. This will **appear** to be the final solution sought so earnestly by Adolf Hitler… the annihilation of the Jewish people. It will **appear** to be the long-awaited fulfillment of the world's anti-Semitic dreams…The Jew haters will relish the thought… "At last, mankind will be rid of that horrid blemish… that ulcerous cancer on humanity… at last, ***the Jews*** will be annihilated!"

And from a human perspective … And from the world's perspective… It will look like it's finally going to happen. It will look like the Muslim nations are finally going to kill all the Jews. I mean, how can they possibly lose? With the leadership of the great nuclear powered nation of Russia and this great host of Muslim nations, how can they possibly lose this war?

The answer is found in just two words… "But God". But God is going to use this war to demonstrate to the entire world that He is still on His throne… and there is nothing beyond His abilities.

The world was astounded by the routing that Israel gave the Arabs in the Six Day War. But this is going to the ONE DAY War… maybe even the ONE HOUR War.

Ezek 38:18 – *And it shall come to pass at the same time when Gog shall come against the land of Israel, saith the Lord GOD, that **my fury shall come up in my face.***
*19 For in my jealousy and in the **fire of my wrath** have I spoken, Surely in that day there shall be a great shaking in the land of Israel;*

Ezekiel goes on to describe the awesome devastation that God is going to rain down on this invading Russian-Islamic horde.

Ezek 38:22 - *And I will plead against him with **pestilence and with blood; and I will rain upon him, and upon his bands, and upon the many people that are with him, an overflowing rain, and great hailstones, fire, and brimstone.***
23 Thus will I magnify myself, and sanctify myself; ...

God also says through Ezekiel in vs. 21 that He will cause such confusion among the soldiers that they will begin to fight against one another and *"every man's sword shall be against his brother."*

And what will be the final outcome of this war??? When this massive army makes its way into Israel, God says that He will destroy 5/6ths of the entire invading force… leaving only 1/6th of it to straggle back home, decimated and defeated.

Ezek 39:1-5 – *"Therefore, thou son of man, prophesy against Gog, and say, Thus saith the Lord GOD; Behold, I am against thee, O Gog, the chief prince of Meshech and Tubal:*
2 And I will turn thee back, and leave but the sixth part of thee, and will cause thee to come up from the north parts, and will bring thee upon the mountains of Israel:
3 And I will smite thy bow out of thy left hand, and will cause thine arrows to fall out of thy right hand. [Weapons will malfunction!]
4 Thou shalt fall upon the mountains of Israel, thou, and all thy bands, and the people that is with thee: I will give thee unto the ravenous birds of every sort, and to the beasts of the field to be devoured.
5 Thou shalt fall upon the open field: for I have spoken it, saith the Lord GOD."

God Does the Impossible
Notice the way God defeats these nations. He does something that only He could do (certainly, not the tiny nation of Israel). And, this is the way God works. He takes an impossible situation and performs that which man can not do. Otherwise, if what He did was common to men, then men would take the credit for it. Only God will be able to save Israel from such an onslaught. No doubt, Israel, with her mighty military could put up a good fight, but such an invasion led by Russia with so many other Muslim nations would be too much for Israel to handle. So, God steps into an impossible situation and saves the day!

WHERE the victory will be won
Another point to make here is the *place* where God defeats Gog and his forces. It seems that God waits until the last minute to intervene because He destroys them as they enter **the mountains of Israel.**

God doesn't destroy them as they are gathering their forces in their homeland. Nor does He destroy them as they are making their way down to Israel. No. God waits until they are IN Israel… And THEN He makes His move. It's at that time when the situation seems the most bleak… When all hope is lost… When every other human resource has been exhausted, THEN the God of Israel comes to her rescue.

We should learn a lesson here.
Whatever your struggle is today… Whatever burden Satan is using to crush you… If you've lost all hope of your problem ever being resolved… DON'T GIVE UP HOPE!

God often waits till the last minute to turn the tables and convert the curse into a blessing! THAT'S HIS WAY!!
He's never late.
He's always on time.
But He's seldom early.

Lesson 3 Quiz

1. "Gog" is not a proper name, but rather it is a _____ for the supreme leader of the nation of _____.

2. According to Gen. 10:1-2, Magog was the son of _____ who was the son of _____.

3. Gen. 38:15 - *"And thou shalt come from thy place out of the _____ _____, thou, and many people with thee..."*

4. The first nation listed in the coalition of nations in Ezek. 38:5 is _____ which is the modern nation of _____.

5. T or F   Today (2014) Iran has strong diplomatic relations with Russia.

6. _____ _____ is the current president of Russia.

7. The nation listed as Ethiopia in Ezek. 38 is actually a reference to the modern nation of _____ south of Egypt.

8. Ezek. 39:2 says that God will kill all but _____ (what part) of the invading forces on the mountains of Israel.

9. God uses a metaphor by saying that He will bring Gog of Magog down to Israel by putting _____ in their _____.

10. T or F   God will intervene in this war by destroying the invading forces before they ever get started good.

Lesson 3 Quiz Answers

1. title, Russia (or Magog)

2. Japheth, Noah

3. north parts

4. Persia, Iran

5. True

6. Vladimir Putin

7. Sudan

8. 1/6th

9. hooks, jaws

10. False. He will destroy them on the mountains of Israel.

Lesson 4

The War of Gog of Magog – Part 2
Ezekiel 38-39
(Footnotes for this lesson are at the end of Lesson 5)

So far, we've discussed **WHO** it is that's going to come against Israel. And, we talked about **WHAT** the result of that invasion is going to be when God steps in to save Israel. He will utterly destroy those invading armies as they enter into northern Israel, leaving only $1/6^{th}$ of them alive to return home and tell the story about the mighty hand of the God of Israel.

But now let's look at two more questions about this prophecy…

Why Is God Going To Do This?
First, we must ask **WHY** is this going to happen. And then, finally, (and maybe most importantly for us today) we'll look at **WHEN** this invasion is going to occur.

When we search the Scriptures for an answer as to **WHY** this invasion will occur, we can find at least three reasons…

(1) God will MAKE it happen in order to bring glory to Himself.

God said in 38:4 that He Himself would bring Gog and his partner nations to the land of Israel: *"I will turn thee back, and put hooks into thy jaws, and **I will bring thee forth**,…"*

As though they are being drug by hooks in their jaws, they will descend upon Israel. The invisible, super-natural hand of God will force them to come upon Israel because it is all part of His omnipotent plan to bring glory unto Himself.

When God steps in at the last moment to save Israel from this massive invasion, the nations of **the world will sit back in utter disbelief** at what their eyes have seen. This great act of salvation will stupefy the world and they will realize that there truly is a God in Heaven that governs the affairs of men and nations (Dan. 4:17).

(2) (And we may put this as a footnote to reason #1… If God is MAKING it happen, then this will be the means He employs)
    Gog will make this invasion to loot and steal the wealth of Israel.

Ezek 38:10-12 - *"Thus saith the Lord GOD; It shall also come to pass, that at the same time shall things come into thy mind, and thou shalt think an evil thought:*
11   And thou shalt say, I will go…
*12   **To take a spoil, and to take a prey**; to turn thine hand upon the desolate places that are now inhabited, and upon the people that are gathered out of the nations, which have gotten cattle and goods, that dwell in the midst of the land."*

There has been much speculation over the years as to exactly what kind of **"spoil"** in Israel will stir the greed of Gog to make this attack.

(1) Some have said the billions of dollars in minerals found in the Dead Sea could be the treasure Gog desires.

(2) Another thought is that it could be the great agricultural productivity of Israel. Even though it is a tiny country, agricultural output is among the top in the list of the nations of the world.

But now look at this…
(3) Some have speculated that oil will be discovered in great quantities in Israel and *that* is what Gog will want. Well, so far this has not happened. There have been a few small oil discoveries made in Israel in the last decade, but nothing that really would make her energy independent. In 2006,

The Jerusalem Post
Oct 4, 2006 18:57 | Updated Oct 4, 2006 21:02

Report: Oil discovered in Dead Sea area

By JPOST.COM STAFF

Oil has been discovered in the Dead Sea area, Dr. Eli Tenenbaum, an official from Genco, the national company responsible for drilling in the region, reported on Wednesday. Tenenbaum stated that the amount of oil could reach commercial levels.

But Israel still has to import about 98% of her oil.
But now, let me show you something that presents a much more desirable resource for Russia to long for…

Oil in Israel
Israel Discovers Huge Natural Gas Field

January 18, 2009 by admin

Noble Energy has discovered "three massive gas fields" just off the coast of Haifa. This field is much richer, the natural gas reservoirs much larger than Noble energy expected. This find alone could be enough natural gas to power Israel's electrical plants and supply it's commercial and domestic natural gas needs for the foreseeable future - and still with enough for export to other countries…

Speaking on Army Radio Sunday morning, an exhilarated Yitzhak Tshuva, owner of the Delek Group Ltd, one of the owners of the well, called the discovery "one of the biggest in the world," promising that the find would present a historic land mark in the economic independence of Israel.

"I have no doubt that this is a holiday for the State of Israel. We will no longer be dependent [on foreign sources] for our gas, and will even export. We are dealing with **inconceivably huge quantities**; Israel now has a solution for the future generations," Tshuva added.

This gas field became known as the **Tamar 1** field and is reported to contain 10 trillion cubic feet of natural gas [6]... enough for Israel's needs for at least 25-30 years (and that's a conservative estimate)!

One year later (2010), a second gas field was discovered about 29 miles SW of the Tamar field known as the **Leviathan** field which contains an estimated 22 trillion cubic feet of gas! (over twice as large as the Tamar). With some smaller discoveries in the area, Israel's offshore natural gas discoveries are estimated at 40 tcf, enough to supply them for many decades to come! In fact, Israel now has enough natural gas in reserve to become a major EXPORTING nation of gas. Of course, the other nations of the Middle East and northern Africa all have huge reserves of oil and gas. So, it makes sense that Israel will try to sell her excess gas to Europe.

Now, guess who is a major natural gas exporting country to Europe... **RUSSIA**. In fact, about 40% of the EU's natural gas comes from Russia. And almost all of that gas is transported to Europe through pipelines that run from Russia through the Ukraine.

In 2009, Russia's economy was in desperate need of a cash infusion, so they decided to jack up the price of the natural gas that they were exporting to Ukraine. But the Ukrainians refused to pay the higher prices. So, Russia just cut off the supply.

Look at this NY Times report dated Jan. 1, 2009:

The New York Times

Russia Cuts Off Gas Deliveries to Ukraine

Published: January 1, 2009

MOSCOW — In the face of mounting economic troubles, Russia cut off deliveries of natural gas to Ukraine on Thursday after Ukraine rejected the Kremlin's demands for a sharp increase in gas prices…

Plagued by the sharp fall in oil prices, Russia has been scrambling to make up the revenue shortfall as prices have slipped below $40 a barrel. Gazprom [Russia's gas company], too, is heavily in debt and sinking along with the energy market…

Later Thursday, Gazprom's chief executive raised the asking price to $418 per 1,000 cubic meters from $250, saying that Ukraine had missed its chance to accept the lower rate. [They had initially raised their price from $200 to $250… and then raised it up to $418 per 1000 cubic meters.]

The shutoff at the peak of the heating season carried more than financial overtones; it is the most confrontational move by Russia toward a neighboring country since the August war in Georgia.

This all happened right in the middle of winter and caused some serious energy shortages in the Ukraine. But it didn't just hurt the Ukraine. Remember, most of that gas passes through Ukraine into Europe.

Voice of America News (VOAnews.com)

Ukraine, Russia Pricing Dispute Halts Russian Gas Exports to Europe

By Barry Wood - Washington - *07 January 2009*

The ongoing dispute over transit fees and pricing has halted Russian natural gas exports **to Europe**.

Ukraine and Russia blame each other for the disruption that has curtailed vital gas deliveries to several European countries, including Hungary, Romania, Austria, Slovakia and the Czech Republic. Amid freezing temperatures and usage restrictions, the Japanese automaker Suzuki says it is halting production at its Hungarian affiliate.

The European Union says it is being held hostage to a bilateral dispute and is demanding an immediate resolution of the matter. On Wednesday, German Chancellor Angela Merkel expressed displeasure in telephone conversations with Russia's Prime Minister Vladimir Putin and Ukraine's Prime Minister Yulia Timoshenko. **Germany gets some 37 percent of its natural gas from Russia, 80 percent of that through pipelines that transit Ukraine.**

Now, with a lot of pressure from the Europeans, they eventually worked out a deal to turn the gas valves back on. But just remember this... Russia NEEDS to export all that gas into Europe. However, their pipelines go through Ukraine.

Now, look at this article from the Wall Street Journal:

The Wall Street Journal

- JANUARY 13, 2009

Russia Will Restart Gas Exports to EU

By MARC CHAMPION and JOHN W. MILLER

Russia agreed to restart gas exports to the European Union via Ukraine on Tuesday morning, potentially ending supply cuts that have stoked concerns over the Continent's energy security and left tens of thousands of Europeans without central heat in freezing temperatures.

Further stoppages are possible, EU and Russian officials said, because disputes remain over which side -- Moscow or Kiev -- should provide the gas volumes needed to pump Russia's exports to the EU, as well as over what price Ukraine should pay for its own gas imports from Russia.

Now, add to this picture... Israel... who has all of this new-found gas to export. And guess who they're planning to export it to???

Greece Launches Eastern Mediterranean Pipeline

Athens, Mar 10, 2014 (Prensa Latina) - Greece today started the Eastern Mediterranean Pipeline project with the launching of a tender to assess the feasibility of the program promoted by the Public Natural Gas Supply Corporation of Greece (DEPA) in collaboration with Cyprus" Ministry of Energy.

According to the original design, the pipeline could carry 8 billion cubic meters a year and **it will stretch from Israel's Leviathan natural gas field to Greece and onto European markets.**

How do you think Russia will feel about this competition from Israel in the European gas markets? Could Israel's gas fields be the prey and spoil that Gog of Magog (Russia) desires to possess? Well, we'll have to wait and see. But one thing is for sure... This new gas discovery in Israel (and possibly future oil discoveries) sure makes it a lot more attractive to the greedy desires of Russia.

All of these gas fields lie in what is called the Levant Basin which covers the eastern end of the Mediterranean Sea and the nations in that area. Most geologists will agree that "where there is gas, there is oil". And it has been estimated by the US Geological Survey that there is 1.7 billion barrels of recoverable oil in the Levant. [4]

Along the Israel shoreline, it is believed that that oil lies beneath the recently discovered gas fields, at depths to which technology only in recent years has advanced enough to reach it. Exploration efforts are now underway to drill down to it. [5]

(3) A third reason for Gog and his partner nations to invade Israel is based upon what we have already demonstrated. The nations joining with Russia to make this invasion are MUSLIM nations. So the prevailing reason for the attack may just be because of **the hatred that the Muslims have for the Jews (at least for all the nations except Russia).**

Everyday since Israel declared her independence on May 14, 1948, she has had to fight for her survival. In three major all-out wars, she has been attacked by neighboring Arab Muslim nations:

(1) In 1948, she fought her **War of Independence** against five Arab nations... a war that no one thought she could win... but she did.

(2) In the **Six Day War of 1967**, she was outnumbered 40 to 1 in soldiers...
But in just six days, she completely routed three attacking Arab nations, taking the entire Sinai peninsula from Egypt and driving them all the way back to the Suez Canal.
She drove the Jordanians out of Jerusalem and the West Bank back to the Jordan River.

And she drove Syria completely from the strategical Golan Heights. And she accomplished all of that in just SIX DAYS!

(3) In the **Yom Kippur War of 1973**, when she was attacked by surprise on the holiest day of the year, The Day of Atonement, when all of Israel was focused on self affliction and meditation, she was caught completely off guard and unprepared for the surprise attack by Egypt and Syria. But soon she turned the tables and again... against all odds... she routed her enemies and won the war.

Why? Because God said that He would return the Jews to their land and when He did, NO ONE would ever pluck them up again!

Amos 9:15 - *And I will plant them upon their land, and they shall no more be pulled up out of their land which I have given them, saith the LORD thy God.*

Nevertheless, this does not hinder the demonic hatred that Muslims have for Jews and the nation of Israel. And the dramatic rise in world terrorism from the Muslim nations in the last few decades, along with the discovery of oil in their countries that has brought them massive fortunes of wealth, has lifted them from obscurity to the point of becoming a major world power in the 21st century. Thus, even though there has been an intense hatred of the Jews by the Muslims for centuries, it has only been in recent years that they have gained the assets to implement that hatred through death and destruction.

Islam

In the last 1400 years, history has been witness to the spread of this demonic religious belief system that today has ensnared some 1.2 billion people and 29 nations. Make no mistake about it... **Islam** is a demonic religion that is leading literally millions of deceived people to a devil's Hell.

No matter how politically correct it may be to declare it so, Islam is **NOT** a religion of peace that is being hijacked by a handful of radical fanatics. Islam **IS** a religion of the sword that teaches a doctrine of

acceptance or death... conversion or destruction. They are taught from infancy that all non-believers are infidels who must be either converted to Islam or be put to death. This is what their Imams have decreed... This is what their holy book, the Koran, clearly states.

For example:

Sura 9:5 – "Fight and slay the pagans wherever ye find them, and seize them, beleaguer them, lie in wait for them in every stratagem [of war]."

Sura 47:4 – "Therefore, when ye meet the unbelievers, smite them at their necks; at length, when ye have thoroughly subdued them, bind a bond firmly [on them]."

Islam is a religion based solely on works along with the insecure belief that one never knows whether he has performed enough good works to tip the scales in his favor so he can be accepted by Allah. The only positive way to know that one will be granted entry into paradise is by dying in an attempt to kill infidels. This theology has birthed an entire generation of millions who are anxious to fulfill that destiny.

And soon... the national leader of Russia will arouse that generational hatred of those Muslims for the Jewish people... and will use them in an attempt to take over Israel.
Well, just how close are we to that day?

When we talk about all Muslims, the **Shiites** (also referred to as Shi'as) are the more fundamental and typically, the more fanatical form of Islam. Today, Iran is about 89% Shiite Muslim and 9% Sunni. [8] From 2005 until 2013, hardliner Shiite Muslim **Mahmoud Ahmadinejad** was the president of Iran for two terms. Among his other anti-Semitic remarks, he stated publically that Israel should be wiped off the face of the earth and that the Holocaust is a myth.

The Koran teaches that the Muslim "Messiah" (known as the Mahdi) will return to the public domain and lead the Muslims to take control of the entire planet… establishing a kind of Islamic utopia. It is believed that his coming will be in a time of world chaos and confusion. Consequently, the more fanatical Shiites think that such chaos and confusion must be created in order for their Mahdi to return. What better way to accomplish this than to detonate a nuclear bomb on Israel? Two goals would be accomplished… (1) Israel would be destroyed, and (2) world chaos (and perhaps world war) would ensue.

Ahmadinejad is a strict adherent to this theology. In fact, his convictions run even deeper than that. He actually believes that his god "Allah" has chosen him to "prepare the way" for the Mahdi. One might say that he sees himself as the modern day John the Baptist of Islam… the one whom Allah will use to prepare the way for the Mahdi (by creating world chaos). Thus, we understand his unyielding commitment to Iran's nuclear program, which undoubtedly would be used for building nuclear bombs if allowed to advance to that level.

Well, under the present Iranian constitution, a person can only be president for two terms. So, on June 15, 2013 **Hassan Rouhani** was elected a Ahmadinejad's successor. It is said that Ahmadinejad has returned to his previous job as a university professor with the intention of retiring from politics. However, such men, when they've once held such power, are seldom content to walk away from it (just like Vladimir Putin in Russia). Without a doubt, Ahmadinejad will continue to work in Iran's political system and may even find his way back to some top leadership position in the future.

In the mean time, his successor, **Mr. Hassan Rouhani,** a devout Shiite cleric, is continuing in Ahmadinejad's footsteps. Considered by some to be more of a "moderate" in his political views than

Ahmadinejad because he ran for president on a "reformist" campaign platform promoting women's rights and promising renewed international diplomacy, his political career has been heavily directed by the Iranian Supreme Leader, **Ayatollah Ali Khamenei.** In fact, Rouhani was a leader in the struggle against the government of the Shah of Iran prior to the 1979 Iranian Revolution and was arrested many times for making public speeches against the Shah. And his last position before becoming president was that of the appointed representative of Ayatollah Khamenei to the Supreme National Security Council.

It must be remembered that even though the **president** of Iran is very powerful, it is the Supreme Leader of Islam, **the Ayatollah**, who has the ultimate power in Iran. And the president must abide by his decisions. In the case of Rouhani, this is not a conflict because as a cleric himself and an adamant supporter of the Ayatollah, the two work hand in hand.

Israel's Prime Minister Benjamin Netanyahu called Rouhani a *"wolf in sheep's clothing, a wolf who thinks he can pull the wool over the eyes of the international community"* in a speech to the UN General Assembly. [9]

If Ahmadenijad thinks it is his god-given responsibility to destroy the Jews and create world chaos, then Rouhani, as a Muslim cleric would be **even more committed** to this goal… despite his being touted as a "moderate" by the international media. And this same objective is held by literally millions of Iranians and other Muslims around the world.

On April 20, 2008 a group calling itself the Islamic Thinkers Society protested near the Israeli Embassy in Queens, New York. Carrying placards and banners with the Islamic flag flying over the White

House, they shouted:

"Zionists, Zionists You will pay! The Wrath of Allah is on its way!
Israeli Zionists You shall pay! The Wrath of Allah is on its way!
The mushroom cloud is on its way! The real Holocaust is on its way!

...Allah will repeat the Holocaust right on the soil of Israel
Islam will dominate the world
Islam is the only solution.
Another mushroom cloud, right in the midst of Israel!

At one time, the West may have ignored the ranting of such fanatics. But, now as Iran quickly approaches the ability to produce nuclear bombs, it is being taken much more seriously. Rouhani, Ahmadenijad, and the Iranians' belief in this coming Mahdi and their role to prepare the way is so compelling that they may go to any lengths, including a nuclear attack on Israel and/or the United States, to bring about the apocalyptic event that will usher in their messiah.

But, let me stop right here and make a bold statement.
Iran, nor anyone else, is going to drop a nuclear bomb on Israel!

How do we know this? Because Israel is a tiny nation geographically, just slightly smaller than the state of New Jersey. One nuclear detonation in such a small country would leave it in shambles. Although one nuclear bomb may not kill every single person in the country, it would destroy its infrastructure to a point of no return. The country would no longer have the ability to communicate, organize, or recover. It simply could not continue to function as a national entity.

However, such a destruction of Israel is contrary to the Scriptures. The Bible states clearly that Israel will still be a thriving and livable country when Jesus returns at the Second Coming. She will, in fact, be under attack when Jesus returns to save her as the last moment (Zech. 12:1-10).

Of course, Israel is a very secular society today. So her national leaders know very little about the Bible and they probably wouldn't believe it even if they knew what it says. (Benjamin Netanyahu may be the exception to this.)

So, from a purely secular point of view, the thought of radical Iran possessing nuclear bombs is a very threatening situation... one that simply cannot be allowed to happen. As a matter of national survival, Israel believes that she CANNOT allow Iran to possess nuclear bombs, something that Netanyahu has stated emphatically many times. The nuclear plants where Iran is presently enriching the uranium MUST be destroyed before they are able to produce bomb quality materials.

So a much more likely scenario than Iran dropping the bomb on Israel is that Israel will attack Iran to destroy those nuclear power plants where the uranium is being produced to make the nuclear bombs.

The repercussions of such an attack by Israel will be devastating. It's very likely that Iran would call for a coalition of other Muslim nations to mount a counterattack. And maybe, just maybe, Russia would get in on the ruckus. Could this be the beginning of the Gog of Magog War?

So, the motivation in the heart of Gog of Magog (the leader of Russia) to lead the Muslim nations to attack Israel is his desire for the spoils of Israel, perhaps the gas and/or oil reserves. Add to this the hatred that the Muslim nations have for Israel and it is not hard to see how plans for such an attack could develop in the minds of Gog and his minions.

Lesson 4 Quiz

1. Ezek. 38:12 says that Gog will desire to conquer Israel "to take a _____, and to take a _____".

2. T or F   At present (2014), Israel is almost oil self sufficient.

3. The first two major natural gas discoveries offshore of Israel found the _____ field and the _____ field.

4. The oil and gas deposit that covers the eastern Mediterranean Sea is known as the _____ Basin.

5. Russia sells a lot of natural gas to Europe, but most of those pipelines delivering that gas go through the country of _____.

6. About ____% of the European Union's natural gas consumption is imported from Russia.

7. Today, there about _____ Muslims in the world with about ____ nations having a majority of Islamic citizens.

8. Iran is almost totally _____ Muslim (what kind).

9. The current president of Iran is _____ _____. He succeeded _____ _____, the last president of Iran.

10. T or F   According to Scripture, it is possible that Iran will drop a nuclear bomb on Israel one day.

Lesson 4 Quiz Answers

1. spoil, prey

2. False. Israel imports about 98% of her oil.

3. Tamar 1, Leviathan

4. Levant

5. Ukraine

6. 40%

7. 1.2 billion, 29

8. Shi'a (or Shiite)

9. Hassan Rouhani, Mahmoud Ahmadinejad

10. False. One nuclear bomb would destroy Israel and yet the Bible says that she will exist until the day of the Lord's return.

Lesson 5

The War of Gog of Magog – Part 3
Ezekiel 38-39

So far in our discussion of the War of Gog of Magog, we have talked about:
WHO will make this attack on Israel
WHAT God is going to do, and
WHY it will happen (especially the possible motive in the heart of Gog)

But now, this brings us to what may be the most relevant question for us today... **WHEN will this battle take place?**

Ezekiel gives us the first clue to this answer when God declares that it is not something that will happen in Ezekiel's day:

As God is speaking directly to Gog of Magog through Ezekiel, He says in
Ezek 38:8 - "***After many days*** *thou shalt be visited:...*" And then, He goes on to say, "*...**in the latter years** thou shalt come...*"

Then, in
Ezek 38:16 - "*And thou shalt come up against my people of Israel, as a cloud to cover the land; it shall be **in the latter days**, and I will bring thee against my land...*"
which is a term used in the OT to speak of the days leading up to Israel's final restoration in the Messianic Kingdom.

So, the Scriptures are definitely talking about something that is going to happen in the end of the age in those days that will usher in our Lord's Second Coming. Of course, nothing even remotely similar to this massive invasion and miraculous deliverance by God has ever happened in history, so we know that as of today (2014), it is still yet to come.

One thing we know about the time factor is that this invasion will occur when the Jews are gathered in their land again and are existing as a sovereign nation. God says that Gog will come into *"...the land that is brought back from the sword, and is gathered out of many people"* (38:8). This, of course, has already happened since Israel declared her independence on May 14, 1948. And, to this day, the Jewish people are still returning to their homeland from nations all around the earth.

However there is much disagreement as to when this war will be fought, relative to The Tribulation.

There are two main schools of thought on this:

1. BEFORE the Tribulation starts

Proponents of this timing point to two main arguments:

(1) Ezekiel 38: 11, 14 says, *"And thou shalt say, I will go up **to the land of unwalled villages; I will go to them that are at rest, that dwell safely** ["batach"* in Hebrew]**, all of them dwelling without walls, and having neither bars nor gates,**...
14. *Therefore, son of man, prophesy and say unto Gog, Thus saith the Lord GOD; In that day **when my people of Israel dwelleth safely**, shalt thou not know it?"*

They point out that the original Hebrew (*"batach"*) means "security". So, this does NOT mean that Israel will be secure because they are at peace, but because of their confidence in their own strength, just as they are today. And, today their *kibbutzim* (villages) are no longer walled for protection.

(2) After the war is over, Ezek. 39:9 says that Israel will burn their enemies' weapons for seven years. Because we know that Antichrist will take control of Jerusalem at the midpoint of the Tribulation and begin his persecution of the Jews, in the last half of

the Tribulation, the Jews will be fleeing from that persecution. So, they won't be in a situation of collecting and burning those weapons during the last half of the Tribulation. Thus, the seven years of burning weapons would have to start at least three and one half years before the beginning of the seven year Tribulation.

2. IN the first half of the Tribulation

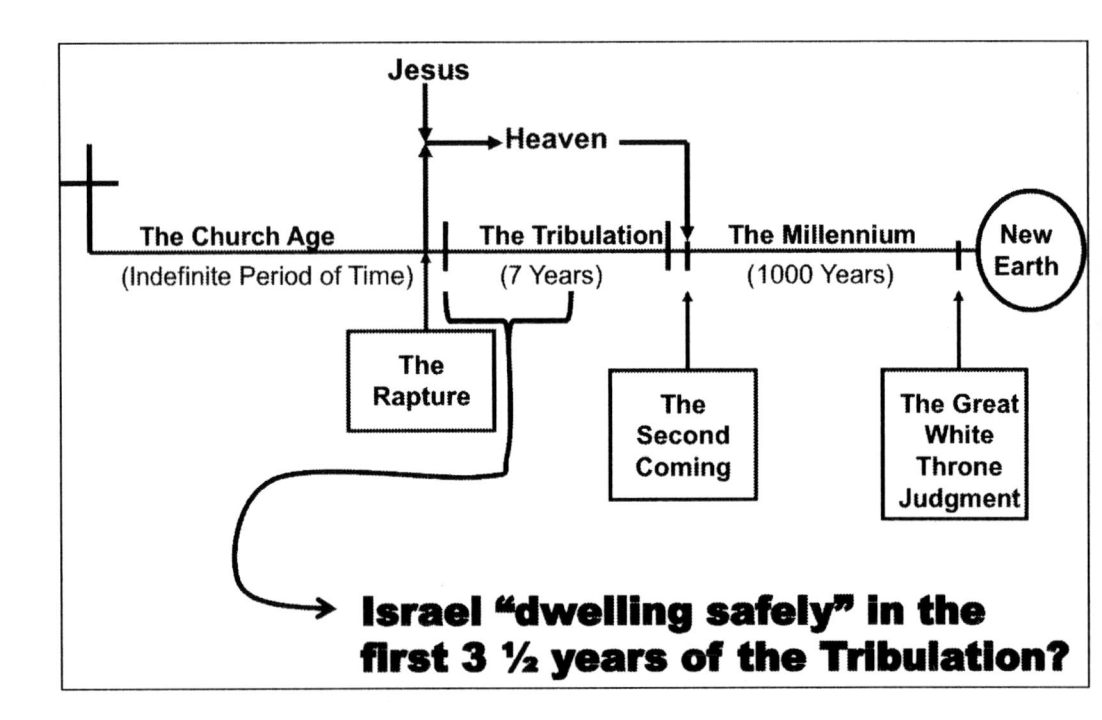

```
                    Jesus
                      ↓
                  → Heaven →
    ┼─────────────────┬──────────────┬──────○
    The Church Age    The Tribulation  The Millennium   New Earth
    (Indefinite Period of Time)  (7 Years)   (1000 Years)

         The Rapture     The Second Coming    The Great White Throne Judgment

    → Israel "dwelling safely" in the
       first 3 ½ years of the Tribulation?
```

Proponents of this view believe that the only time when Israel will enjoy a time of peace and safety (not counting the time of the Millennium) will be in the first half of the Tribulation when she will be living under the security of the seven year covenant of the Antichrist. For this reason, they believe the Magog War will happen in the first half of the Tribulation.

There are other timing factors to consider, such as (1) the Jews will be back in their land, and (2) it will happen in the "latter years" (38:8). But I think both of these scenarios satisfy these requirements.

Both arguments are convincing. Thus, I would conclude that the Magog War will probably be fought *either* just BEFORE or just AFTER the Tribulation begins. In other words, though we cannot pinpoint the exact timing, it would be safe to say that it will happen *somewhere around the start of the Tribulation* (either just before or after).

Other Recent Developments

Other recent developments seem to be setting the stage for the coming war of Gog of Magog as well. One of those is the character and recent actions of today's Russian president...

(1) Russia's Leader

Today, Russia's president is an egotistical, strongly decisive, aggressive, ex-KGB (Russia's secret service) agent, leader named **Vladimir Putin.** Because he is the leader of Russia, in that sense, he is "Gog of Magog". But is he THE Gog of Magog spoken of in Ezekiel 38? Of course, only when this prophecy is fulfilled will we know the answer to that. However, what we CAN say is that there has been a lot of geopolitical "stage setting" going on in the last decade for the Magog prophecy's fulfillment and Vladimir Putin has been right in the middle of all of it.

After Putin served the maximum number of consecutive terms as president allowed by the Russian constitution (two), he turned over the office to Dmitry Medvedev. It is believed by many that Medvedev was hand picked by Putin and that he was controlled by Putin during his time as president. Just one day after Medvedev took office as president, Putin was appointed as Prime Minister, maintaining his political dominance. Then, after just one term out of the presidency, he was re-elected in 2012 and remains president today.

Without a doubt, Vladimir Putin's personality, aggressiveness, and strong fisted control in Russia certainly make him a good candidate for being the one who could fulfill the role of Gog from the land of Magog!

(2) Georgia

Georgia is the tiny nation along the southern border of Russia between the Caspian and Black seas… along the Caucacus mountain range. It is also one of the ex-Soviet bloc nations that broke away and declared their independence in 1991 around the time of the collapse of the USSR, so they've not had good relations with the "mother country" of Russia ever since.

Within Georgia, there are two regions (South Ossetia and Abkhazia) that have a number of "separatists" who believe they should have their own independence from Georgia and would prefer to become part of Russia. And, in their efforts to make that happen, they've received a substantial amount of help from Russia for reasons obvious to those who understand the prophecies of Ezek. 38-39.

In July, 2008 fighting broke out between the "separatists" and the Georgian government. Immediately, Russia moved its military forces into Georgia to help in the fight of these regions to break away from Georgia. Consequently, a war broke out in South Ossetia between Russia and Georgia. After several weeks of fighting, a truce was brokered by the European Union and Russia withdrew, leaving only a **"peace keeping"** force behind.

The truth is… Russia still has control of the area of South Ossetia in Georgia. But why is that so important and what connection does it have with the Gog of Magog prophecy?

Well, just like a giant wall, the Caucasus Mountain Range stretches about 1200 kilometers from the Black Sea in the NW to the Caspian Sea in the SE. This range of mountains effectively sits like an East-West wall between these two seas, obstructing travel in a north-south direction.

However, in South Ossetia, there is a 12,000 ft. long tunnel (2 ¼ miles) through the mountains built by the Soviets in 1985. It's called the "Roki Tunnel" and it is effectively the ONLY way to travel through the mountain range. If Russia wanted to move its military southward through the Caucasus Mountains, it would **_have to have_** access to the Roki Tunnel. NOW, with their control of South Ossetia, they have that access.

Wikipedia Encyclopedia states:
"The tunnel has been important throughout the Georgian-Ossetian conflict... Since the Russian authorities blocked the Kazbegi-Verkhni Lars customs checkpoint in June 2006 **the Roki Tunnel has been the only available road route from Russia to South Ossetia***. The tunnel was used as a supply route for the Russian military during the 2008 South Ossetia War."* [7]

The Russians can now move through the Roki Tunnel… through Georgia…through Turkey (one of the Magog coalition nations)… through Syria and into Israel. Before July, 2008, this was not possible! This is also motive for Russia to support the government in Syria from being overthrown. In any case, **the Russians now have a straight southward path to Israel in which they can move their land forces down to "the mountains of Israel" (39:2).**

(3) Turkey

Another major development that has happened in the last few years involves the country of Turkey. *"Since its foundation as a republic in 1923, Turkey has developed a strong tradition of secularism."* [10] That is, it has been ruled by a secular (non-religious) government that allowed it to have strong foreign relations with western nations.

After the fall of the Ottoman Empire in World War I, Turkey became increasingly integrated with the West through membership in organizations such as the Council of Europe and NATO. They began full membership negotiations with the European Union in 2005, having been an associate member since 1963, but they have not yet been granted membership into the EU. This is in part due to the fact that Turkey is 99.8% Muslim [11] and Europe, even though it has long departed its Christian roots in practice, still views itself as a society with a Christian heritage.

So the question must be raised… How is it possible that Turkey, with its strong ties and relations with the West, will join a coalition of nations headed by Russia and Iran? For years, it has looked like this was politically impossible.

But remember, even though Turkey's government has prided itself for decades on its purely secular government, over 99% of the people are devout Muslims. So, in July, 2007, for the first time in its post-Ottoman history, an Islamic-based party won 46% of the votes in the parliamentary elections and lead to the inauguration of a strictly Islamic Prime Minister… **Mr. Recep Tayyip Erdogan.**

New York Times

Ruling Party in Turkey Wins Broad Victory

By SABRINA TAVERNISE
Published: July 23, 2007

ISTANBUL, Monday, July 23 — The Islamic-inspired governing party of Prime Minister Recep Tayyip Erdogan won a larger-than-expected victory in nationwide parliamentary elections on Sunday, taking close to half the total vote in a stinging rebuke to Turkey's old guard [the secular government].

With nearly all the votes counted, the Justice and Development Party led by Mr. Erdogan won 46.6 percent of the vote, according to Turkish election officials, far more than the 34 percent the party garnered in the last election, in 2002.

So, for the first time since its founding in 1923, the government of Turkey is being controlled by Muslim politicians who lean strongly in favor of a political system based on Islamic law.

Under the leadership of Mr. Erdogan, in May, 2010, Turkey supported a flotilla of ships that left her port supposedly loaded with humanitarian aid for the people of Gaza. However, Israel had established a naval blockade of Gaza to prevent arms from being smuggled in that would be used against Israel. The Israeli government proposed bringing the ships into the port city of Ashdod to inspect the cargo, but the ship's activists refused. So, Israeli commandos boarded the ships in international waters where they were met with violence and nine of the activists were killed by Israeli soldiers. This incident created a great international outcry and an almost complete severance of relations between Israel and Turkey. Turkey not only expelled Israel's ambassador, but also withdrew their ambassador in Israel.

After Israel's Prime Minister Benjamin Netanyahu gave an official apology to Turkey for the incident, tensions between the two nations were eased, but to date have never been fully restored. **As mentioned earlier, Turkey is named as one of the coalition nations in the Magog War against Israel** (Gomer, Togarmah, Meshech, and Tubal in Ezek. 38:2,6).

So, it is easy to see how Turkey is turning from its historically western political ties to a more eastern direction. Today, their ties with Russia and other eastern Muslim nations is growing stronger while their ties with Israel, the United States, and other western nations are gradually being severed. With the strict Muslim leadership of President Erdogan, Turkey's relationship with Israel has been anything but amiable.

Also, in May, 2010, Russia signed an agreement with Turkey to build their first nuclear power plant in Akkuyu, Turkey. Plans are for the plant construction to begin in 2016 with operation start-up to follow in 2020. So, it is easy to see how Russia is using their nuclear technology to build stronger relations with Turkey, just as they have done in Iran.

(4) Ukraine
Ukraine is one of the eastern European break away nations from the old Soviet USSR. To say the least, it has suffered strained relations with Russia since its declaration of independence in 1991.

As discussed earlier, about 40% of Europe's natural gas supply comes from Russia. And almost all of that gas is transported through pipelines through the Ukraine. So, the Ukrainians have control over how much of that Russian gas makes it to the European Union. To say the least, Russia is not happy with this arrangement. Remember that most of those pipelines were built when Ukraine was still a part of the Soviet Union and Russia had control of the country. But after the collapse of the USSR and Ukraine's subsequent declaration of independence, a treaty was signed between the two countries in 2010 called the **Russian Ukrainian Naval Base for Gas Treaty** allowing Russia's lease on her naval facilities in the Crimean peninsula of Ukraine to be extended 25 years in exchange for discounted rates on the Russian natural gas provided to Ukraine.

Russian maintains a massive, strategic warm water naval base in Crimea on the Black Sea. With her northern ports iced in for the better part of the year, this location gives them year round access to the Mediterranean Sea and thus, the oceans of the world. It is of utmost importance for Russia to maintain this base of operation. So, she used her gas supply to Ukraine to strong-arm them into the treaty that allows Russia to have its base in Crimea.

In Nov., 2013, massive protests broke out in the Ukrainian capital city of Kiev against the government's moves away from its ties with the European Union, which was being dictated to them by Vladimir Putin through Ukrainian president, Viktor Yanukovych. On 21 February 2014, under pressure of the protestors, President Yanukovych fled Kiev. An interim government was established the next day and an interim president was appointed. The United States and the European Union recognized this new government, but Russia strongly condemned the new Ukrainian government as illegal and accused the US and the EU as being the ones responsible for it.

Beginning on Feb. 26, just five days after Yanukovych left office,

Russia sent her army into the southern peninsula of Ukraine called Crimea and took control of it. Putin, claiming that he was acting as the protector of the mostly Russian speaking Crimeans, later organized a referendum in which it was reported that 97% of the people of Crimea voted in favor of being annexed by Russia. Even though the international community has rejected this, Russia has blatantly invaded, controlled, and annexed Crimea away from Ukraine into the Russian Federation. **In March, 2014, Russia unilaterally terminated the Russian Ukrainian Naval Base for Gas Treaty.** She no longer needs an agreement with Ukraine to have her naval base in Crimea. However, Ukrainian control of Russian gas to Europe still remains a difficult issue in the two countries' relations.

Next, Russian military forces have been amassed along the eastern Ukraine and Russian borders which Russia reports as "normal" military exercises. Numerous reports of Russian special operations soldiers in plain clothing have come from various eastern border districts of Ukraine blending in with separatist nationals who have taken control of a number of government buildings. All appearances indicate that Vladimir Putin is staging an eventual military move into mainland Ukraine against international, UN, NATO, US and EU warnings.

So the question remains… Will Vladimir Putin continue his aggression and move to take all of Ukraine? And, if he does, what will be the response of the United States and the rest of the western nations?

It is my opinion that it is only a matter of time before Putin attempts to take all of the Ukraine. His strong, arrogant and aggressive personality will not allow him to be satisfied with just a portion of the Ukraine and he doesn't like the idea of not controlling the Ukrainian pipelines that carry Russian gas into Europe. Russian control of Ukraine will definitely further identify with the Magogites who were the Scythians that roamed that area of the world.

(5) Russia and the Nations of Islam

Along with Russia's aggression in Georgia and Ukraine, they have steadily courted stronger relations with the Muslim nations of the world.

- Russia has been the only non-Muslim country to accept the Hamas terrorist organization in Gaza as a legitimate government.
- Vladimir Putin made a first time ever state visit to Iran to discuss national relations with Iran's Ahmadinejad.
- Russia has helped Iran to build its nuclear power plant at Busheir and has sold hi-tech military weapons to Iran, including some very sophisticated anti-aircraft missiles.
- Russia has consistently supported the Syrian government of Bashar al-Assad and has warned against any military intervention by the United States.
- Russian maintains a naval base in Tartus, Syria.

Russia's political maneuvering and diplomacy in the last decade has built the strong national ties to duplicate the exact coalition of nations described in Ezekiel 38-39. The stage is set for the "Magog nations" to attack Israel!

So, let's review quickly…

Fact #1 - The Gog of Magog attack will be made by Russia and a coalition of Muslim nations either just before or in the first half of the Tribulation when Israel is dwelling safely (securely) in her land.

Fact#2 - Iran's fanatical Muslim leadership is determined to build a nuclear arsenal.

Fact #3 – In pursuit of that goal, Iran is thumbing its nose at the western world and building stronger ties with Russia.

Fact #4 - Israel believes that if no one else does it (and it doesn't look like anyone else will) that they MUST stop Iran from producing a nuclear weapon. Such an attack could be the spark that causes a retaliatory attack by Russia and the Magog coalition of nations.

Fact #5 - The political and economic ties between Russia, Iran, Turkey, and other Muslim nations listed in Ezekiel 38 is growing stronger every day.

Fact #6 - With the recent discovery of the huge reservoir of natural gas in Israel, they certainly now have a "spoil" that Gog of Magog (Russia) will want.

Fact #7 - Vladimir Putin, the president of Russia, has the exact personality and character of the man who could become "Gog of Magog".

Fact #8 - With Russia's control of the Roki Tunnel into northern Georgia, they now have an open alleyway between the Black and Caspian seas, through the Caucasus Mountain range, down to Israel.

Fact #9 - After over nine decades since its establishment as a secular government in 1923, Turkey has elected a strong Muslim Prime Minister in 2007 who has led them away from their western ties to stronger relations with Russia and the other Muslim nations.

Fact #10 - Russia's recent invasion into Ukraine further identifies them as the Magogites described in Ezekiel 38 and exponentially increases the tension between them and the US, Israel, and the West.

Fact #11 - Under the leadership of Vladimir Putin, Russia has built strong commercial and political ties with all the Muslim nations identified by Ezekiel as the coalition that will join Russia to attack Israel in fulfillment of the prophecy of Gog of Magog in Ezekiel 38-39.

It certainly appears that the geopolitical stage is set TODAY for the fulfillment of the prophecy of the war of Gog of Magog. But let me say very clearly and plainly…

NO ONE knows exactly how all of this going to play out. God has given us much information about this attack from Gog of Magog, but exactly what developments will lead up to it actually happening is something that only God knows.

I have given you some information that seems to point to its fulfillment on the horizon. What I want you to see in all of this is that **the stage is set NOW** for it to happen…
And as Christians, this means we need to be looking up!

God told the prophet Daniel after giving him much information about these last days of the age that will bring in the true Messiah, Jesus Christ…

*"…Go thy way, Daniel: for the words are closed up and sealed till **the time of the end**.*

10 …the wicked shall do wickedly: and none of the wicked shall understand; but the wise shall understand." (Daniel 12:9-10)

And Jesus said concerning the signs that will precede His coming,

*"And when these things **begin** to come to pass, then look up, and lift up your heads; for your redemption draweth nigh."* Luke 21:28

----

(1)   Chuck Missler, <u>The Magog Invasion,</u> (Little Rock: The Western Front, LTD, 1996) p. 30-31
(2)   http://christiananswers.net/dictionary/meshech.html?zoom_highlight=meshech
(3)   http://christiananswers.net/dictionary/tubal.html?zoom_highlight=tubal
(4)   http://www.usgs.gov/science/cite-view.php?cite=2383
(5)   http://www.bloomberg.com/news/2013-07-17/israel-s-deepest-well-targets-1-5-billion-barrels-of-oil.html
(6)   http://www.nobleenergyinc.com/Exploration/Recent-Discoveries-130.html
(7)   http://en.wikipedia.org/wiki/Roki_tunnel
(8)   http://en.wikipedia.org/wiki/Islam_in_Iran
(9)   http://www.cnn.com/2013/10/01/world/meast/israel-netanyahu-iran/
(10) http://en.wikipedia.org/wiki/Turkey#Foreign_relations
(11) https://www.cia.gov/library/publications/the-worldfactbook/geos/tu.html

Lesson 5 Quiz

1. There are two main schools of thought about WHEN the War of Gog of Magog will take place. Some put it _____ the start of the Tribulation and others put it in the _____ _____ of the Tribulation.

2. T or F   In one sense, Vladimir Putin is Gog of Magog.

3. A strategic tunnel runs through the Caucasus Mountain range with the nation of _____ at the north end and the nation of _____ at the south end. The name of this tunnel is the _____ Tunnel.

4. The modern nation of Turkey was founded in _____ with a _____ type of government.

5. The current president of Turkey is _____ _____ and he has led them towards a government that is based more on Islamic law called _____ law.

6. In 2010, an international incident occurred when Turkey sent a flotilla of ships loaded with humanitarian aid to try to break Israel's naval blockade around _____.

7. In 2010, Russia and Ukraine signed an agreement to allow Russia to maintain its _____ _____ in the southern peninsula of Ukraine on the _____ Sea.

8. In 2014, Russia militarily took control of a peninsula of southern Ukraine called _____.

9. The nation that helped Iran build its first nuclear power plant in the city of Busheir is _____.

10. T or F   Russia has strongly condemned the government of Bashar al-Assad and called for him to step down.

Lesson 5 Quiz Answers

1. before, first half

2. True. In the sense that he is presently the supreme leader of Russia.

3. Russia, Georgia, Roki

4. 1923, secular

5. Recep Erdogan, Sharia

6. Gaza

7. naval base, Black

8. Crimea

9. Russia

10. False. Russia supports Bashar al-Assad and his government in Syria.